Group Games
Social Skills

Group Games
Social Skills

BIRGIT FUCHS

Speechmark

Speechmark Publishing Ltd
Telford Road • Bicester • Oxon OX26 4LQ • United Kingdom

Originally published in German by Don Bosco Verlag München under the title *Spiele fürs Gruppenklima* © Don Bosco Verlag, München 1998

Published in 2002 by
Speechmark Publishing Ltd, Telford Road, Bicester, Oxon OX26 4LQ, UK
www.speechmark.net

© Speechmark Publishing Ltd, 2002

002-5134/Printed in the United Kingdom/1030

British Library Cataloguing in Publication Data

Fuchs, Birgit
  Social skills. – (Group Games)
  1. Social skills in children 2. Group games
  I. Title
  302.1'4'083

ISBN 0 86388 420 2

Contents

About the Author

Birgit Fuchs is from Bobingen in Germany. She is a 'motherly leader' of a family of five. She works as a teacher and is the author of several pedagogical reference books on the subject of 'learning through play'.

Acknowledgement

Thank you to Lilo Seelos, the translator.

Note: The text sometimes refers to the leader or the child as 'he', for the sake of clarity alone.

Games

Learning Games

Introduction

HOW ANGER, RAGE AND DISAPPOINTMENT COME INTO BEING

This book is about improving the social climate in families and groups. When is there trouble in a group? When does a person get annoyed? For example, when they feel unfairly treated or misunderstood. When they are being teased; when too much is expected of them; when they are being attacked, or simply being overlooked. When they have no friends, or when the wrong ones stand by their side, and so on. Bad moods also come into being when too much responsibility is given; when never-ending boredom; lack of space; permanent control, or an environment that provides little stimulation, drastically reduce scope for action.

All these factors can reduce self-confidence, and consequently create fear. Fear, in turn, is a breeding ground for aggression. Aggression can show itself in a number of ways. In one person, it may hide behind arrogance, provocation, mockery and irony, or even physical attacks. Another person may react in a more whiny, over-sensitive manner, or even show signs of phobia.

The reactions are pre-programmed: the trouble-maker is told, 'You again. Well, that was to be expected!' Another may be told for the hundredth time: 'For goodness sake. Pull yourself together. You'll never get anywhere in life.' And then something that makes the situation even worse happens: both become frustrated anew; the potential for aggression is stoked up, and the undesired behaviour is thus reinforced. The vicious circle is completed, and the group climate develops accordingly. Every teacher of a group will find the way out of such a dilemma more easily if they realise that hardly any trouble-maker feels comfortable inside their own skin. They are suffering distress, even though they may vociferously be claiming the opposite.

GAMES CREATE A GOOD BASIS

It follows that the causes of anger and suffering are varied and individually different. Just as diverse are the possibilities of tracking down these causes in order to understand the enigma of human reactions.

This requires the development of social feeling and social intelligence. Keen observation; precise listening, and empathetic communication are fundamental prerequisites for the creation of a stable community and an atmosphere of trust. The aim is a community that recognises the needs and fears of the individual, and approaches them constructively – a group where everyone can trust each other.

The following collection of games shows how this can happen with humour and excitement. It includes numerous ideas about ways in which people can find out more about themselves and others and, while doing this, can share a lot of fun and provide a stable, respectful togetherness.

The games can be utilised in many ways: whether in one's own family, nursery or playgroups, school classes, holiday groups or youth clubs; anyone who works with children, teenagers, or even adults is catered for. Nor does it matter when players of different ages find themselves together for a joint game, because sets of games – with a few exceptions – are not categorised in terms of age-specific contents or abilities, but deal with generally relevant aspects of group life.

AIMS

The games seek to increase awareness of people and things in one's environment, as with order and tidiness games. Different possibilities are demonstrated as to how squabblers can let off steam and still find common ground again. All games involve strengthening the self-confidence of individual members, so that they can stand up to the complex demands of group-dynamic processes. Someone who is looking for game ideas to fend off boredom, which can so easily lead to displeasure, will also find ideas here. In addition, there is a selection of fiddly learning games that show that acquiring knowledge can be fun, and not just for the pupils! And to ensure that the weekend, too, will be a success, another selection offers a colourful game-mix for joint leisure activities.

RULES

All games can be played with no or hardly any materials. Utensils used can nearly all be found in any household or group room. When several participants are involved, it may make sense to determine the number of players, depending on temperament and make-up of the group. The graphics that follow each game title indicate how many players should be involved. Thus 🙎 indicates a game that is suitable for one person, 🙎🙎 a game for partners, and 🙎🙎🙎🙎 a group game. The combination of 1 and 8 makes it clear that the individual becomes active first, and then brings their experiences into a group activity.

The creative drawing up of rules can also be a very funny, profitable endeavour. That is why players themselves should be given the opportunity to do this. However, it is important that it is agreed by all that *no participant must be hurt in any way* through any of the regulations that are made.

Timing is also important to ensure the successful outcome of the games. A reconciliation game, for example, should not follow on immediately after a serious argument: aggressive feelings are still too fresh to be switched off at a command. Tidiness games are different: in this case, a long waiting period would be wrong as, in the meantime, the 'battlefield' may have been cleaned up by someone else.

For games where people are supposed to open up, the arrangement of the environment is as important as the right timing. For example, most people will find it easier to talk in a warm, comfortable room with subdued lighting, than in an impersonal, cold hall under neon light.

Finally, a factor that should not be underestimated for the successful application of the games is the introduction: 'Listen everyone, we are going to play a game …' is often not enough to awaken the desire to play. An informative or mysterious lead-in, maybe disguised as a riddle, can increase the expectation considerably.

So here's to fun, a successful outcome, and a great atmosphere!

Games &
Exercises for
Social Skills

Awareness Games

In any group, many different people come together. Each of them is a unique individual with their own characteristics, views, attitudes, fears and preferences. It is no wonder that there is not always total harmony. Rules that have been drawn up together are supposed to help strengthen a pleasant social climate. So, if everyone has rationally mastered these rules, why is there still friction, serious conflicts, and even escalations?

The simple understanding of rules, requirements, agreements and so on is something that takes place cognitively in the brain. However, the fact that each person is a being with feelings makes the sensible keeping to desired behaviours more difficult, and indeed often impossible. And herein lies a big problem. Young people today know exactly what is expected of them. Societal pressure is enormous in terms of achievement and social adjustment. They have to function in an optimal fashion in order to 'get anywhere in life'. By doing this, people get caught up in a whirl of expectations, own ideals, societal standards, and devastating needs to compete. We belong to a 'head-focused' society, with the threateningly increasing tendency to psychological frailty and helplessness. Because what is left behind during all this working and doing is, in fact, the individual person: who am I, who knows me, who actually listens to me, and who, in the end, can grant me security through their understanding attitude?

Nothing gives people more calm and security than the close dealing with someone they are allowed to be honest with, who, in this case, is interested in the weaknesses and wishes of group members. Everyone needs at least one person with whom they do not have to play an exhausting role, like an actor. Consequently, the first group of activities comprises numerous games to teach optical and social awareness skills. Only looking at a person more closely and listening to them more attentively makes it possible to really get to know them. With this, the diverse masks of the 'muscle-man', the 'cry-baby', the 'untouchable', and so on, can gradually be taken off, because these games require openness on all channels.

1 Idols

We can learn amazing things about our fellow human beings when we find out what idols they are crazy about, or who they model themselves on. Examples are always people who, in some way, represent attractive models. However, a model may appear attractive to one group member, but not to another.

Maybe squeaky-clean Peter really likes that really scruffy and burnt-out pop star precisely because, for him, he embodies a certain measure of casualness. Maybe Peter would really like to swap his school uniform for jeans full of holes.

The idol game will shed some light on this. In this game, all participants turn into their idolised role models – on the outside as well as the inside. Clothes, gear, hair colour (spray that can be washed out), speech, catch-phrases, performances and so on are copied as authentically as possible. Afterwards, the 'celebrities' (and, of course, unknown role models, too) introduce themselves, and tell the group what impresses them most about that person.

Materials: anything that might be useful for dressing up and making up

2 Padded Messages

'It really hurt me when you told me …' Anyone who lives with other people has had experience of this. It is inevitable that people hurt each other during daily interaction. The trick is to think about what we try to achieve with our 'attack'. Do we want to clarify the issue, or do we want to provoke? The following game helps players to become clearer about the different emotional areas of the receiver.

Using cardboard, make a life-sized conversational partner consisting of a head, a huge stomach and rudimentary limbs. Using a felt-tip pen, make a line to divide the stomach into upper and lower portions. Then put the cardboard person outside against a tree, or tape it to the wall of the house.

Now every player dips a ball of cotton wool into water, wrings it out slightly and gets ready to throw. Hitting the cardboard hero on the head means being able to say something to someone's face. Aiming for the upper stomach means hitting someone in the stomach verbally. Hitting the lower stomach equates to a psychological 'hit below the belt'.

Thirty points are given for each hit to the head area, 10 points for the upper stomach and no points for hits below the belt. This is because it is always best to tell the person we are arguing with our objections, as sensitively as possible, but directly to their face, instead of hitting where it hurts even more, and thus triggering yet more aggression.

Materials: cardboard, pens, cotton wool

3) Flash-Check

Two players stand eye-to-eye. They have a minute to study each other thoroughly, and to try to remember as many details as possible.

Their observational and memory skills are then put to the test: both participants turn around 180 degrees, so that they now stand back to back. Do they remember what pattern the other's socks were? Or whether their trousers were blue or black?

The questions about the two participants are worked out by the remaining group members, and called out one at a time.

For each correct answer, a player is allowed to score one observation point.

Rule: The players are given the same number of questions. In addition, each player has one flash-joker which he can use once before he answers a question. He receives 10 points if the correct answer is given.

Materials: paper, pens

4) Mind Reading

When we think we know someone else well, we should be able to estimate their reactions to certain topics reasonably accurately, shouldn't we?

For this game, each participant brings along any items they choose: everyday objects, photographs, headlines or newspaper articles, and so on. Everything is put into a box.

Then the players sit around a table. The person who begins reaches into the box; pulls out one of the pieces, and places it where it is fully visible in the middle of the table. Every person memorises their first association with that object and the other players then take it in turns to try to guess what each person has thought of. The player who comes closest to guessing the association of another player is allowed to note down 10 science points, and is given a round of applause for their mind-reading ability.

Materials: different objects

5 The Anti-Addiction Mime

In the run-up to this game, and without getting into deep psychological debates, assumptions about different forms of addiction should be gathered.

◆ Which forms of addiction do you know?
◆ How do they present themselves?
◆ What side-effects or consequences does addictive behaviour bring with it?
◆ What causes can lead to addiction?

Through this, it will become clear, among other things, that addicts always harm themselves in some way, and thus behave aggressively towards themselves or even towards others.

Now playing cards are made up, using simple symbols to represent known addictions: for example, a bottle for the drinker; a television for the telly-addict; an arcade game for the pinball player, and a cigarette for the smoker.

With all players seated in a circle, the leader shuffles the picture cards and then holds one up. Quick as a flash, players think of substitute activities or actions that could be carried out instead of the addictive behaviour. These alternatives are then portrayed through mime, which the group has to guess.

After this, every player presents their variation again, and mimes are discussed by the whole group.

Tip: After the game, it might be possible to look for one's own, very personal 'first signs of addiction'. These may be addictions that, while not socially unacceptable, may secretly bother the person concerned.

Materials: picture cards

6 Daily Report

In the bustle of modern living, there is hardly any room for reflection. We always seem to be preoccupied by the next appointment, the next plan, project, homework and so on. Yet it is very important to let past events linger on for a little while – perhaps to enjoy them once more, or to evaluate their meaning objectively from a distance. We can think about which of our experiences we want to carry over to a new day, and which should be filed away once and for all today. This ritual is also meaningful for a group because, if the individual builds up too much unresolved stress (positive or negative), others will generally feel that, too.

A daily report during an evening group circle offers each individual 'reporter' the opportunity to once again address or talk about their impressions of the day. Listeners should remain as quiet and – most importantly – as neutral as possible, unless they are directly asked for advice by the 'daily news reporter'.

(7) Body Talk

This game is about empathy and expressiveness. Instead of the mouth, all other body parts are utilised for communicative purposes during 'body talks'. To do this, two partners sit or stand opposite each other. The active 'sender' reaches into a basket of topical cards and picks out one with the following text, for example:

> 'OK Peter!
> Let's have a good look at you.
> How is your tummy?
> I think you have bags under your eyes.
> Do you still eat so many crisps?'

Now the sender tries to portray the message as accurately as possible through mime, so that the other partner has to 'read' the text off their body. Then it is their turn, to 'speechlessly' look for an answer.

Tip 1: The card texts are prepared by the whole group. Each group member invents one or two scenarios, writes them down, and puts the cards into the basket until the next round.

Tip 2: By the way, nonsense texts and silly stories are particularly funny!

Materials: paper, pens, basket or box

8 Group Weather Map

A funny weather map is drawn on a large piece of paper, to demonstrate how today's emotional and social climate has developed within the group: breakfast: sunshine; squabble: rain cloud; hurricane Theo: dark cloud; Suzy Gentle: fuzzy cloud; high: upward-pointing arrow.

In the morning, for example, during a good breakfast, the sun smiled everywhere. Afterwards a few raindrops fell, because of a squabble about where to go for today's outing. Hurricane Theo (the group leader) flared up and raged when he found out that some rascal had put a wet sponge in one of his walking boots. However, through the mild blowing of the wind (Suzy Gentle), the group had calmed down again by the evening. During the preparations for the camp-fire, a large (mood) high was already approaching.

Tip: Drawn forecasts for the whole weather situation for the following day can also be good fun, especially as certain turbulences sometimes really can be predicted.

Materials: large sheets of paper, pens

9 What Does a Face Tell You?

Faces are cut out from magazines, newspapers, brochures and so on, and collected for the next group meeting. Each member presents their collection of faces, and reports their impressions with regard to the different facial features and expressions.

Someone fixes particularly distinctive photos on to a pin-board and, in a small competition, the best speech bubble can be suggested. Soon, even younger group members will develop a more differentiated perceptive faculty, and will better understand the saying: 'A face speaks volumes'.

Materials: old newspapers, magazines, scissors

10 Group Stew

Here we imagine the whole group or family is the finished dish, and its members are the ingredients for a delicious recipe! Each participant notes down on a piece of paper the quantity and weight details, specifying how they personally see the individual group members being represented. For example, Anna writes:

> Smith Family
> 1 kilo Daddy
> half a kilo Mummy
> half a kilo John
> 100g Anna

In comparison, we have Mrs Smith's estimation:

> Smith Family
> 1 kilo John
> 1 kilo Anna
> 100g Daddy
> 100g Mummy

So now the surprise is perfect! Anna regards herself as the weakest element. But Mum feels like that about herself. And we will see what the remaining recipe suggestions from Dad and John reveal. It is high time to think together about why, and for how long and how often a group member feels particularly disadvantaged.

Materials: paper, pens

11 The Wish Book

 The conception of a common wish book can bring home to some group members that someone is not necessarily happy just because they have new trainers, or because the sun is shining.

In the wish book, everyone who belongs to the group can express anonymously on a piece of paper their secret wishes, desires or worries. The pieces of paper are hole-punched, and filed in a ring binder. This ring binder is freely available at a particular place.

Tip: The use of a typewriter or computer is ideal. Without either of these, it will be easy to trace a particular author by their handwriting. Anonymity is important, because everyone reading the entries should be allowed to think about who the matter of concern may relate to. Also, even the strongest and bravest of people may summon up the courage to admit to his little worries.

Materials: ring binder, paper, typewriter or computer

12 The Advertising Trap

In a community, it is important to be able to differentiate one's own opinion from those of the others. The following playful activity can sharpen the perception for objective judgement. Magazines, newspapers and television adverts are searched for a particular article – for example, soap. A number of makes of soap are noted down, bought and paid for from the group kitty. During a group test, everyone undergoes a two-minute thorough cleansing of their hands, each using a different make of soap.

The result proves that despite considerable price differences, everybody now has clean hands. So what is it that tempts people to buy this or that product? How are the advertising slogans constructed? Which words and pictures manipulate particularly strongly? How can individuals protect themselves? How can they defend themselves against being taken advantage of; being talked into doing something silly, or generally being controlled by other people?

The 'advertising trap' shows such links clearly, and danger recognised is danger averted.

Materials: magazines, newspapers, diverse materials

13   The Blob Family

Within a group, every person represents a certain 'mood atmosphere'. We know, for example, that Sally's moods change frequently; Tom is a model of happiness; Tina potters about determinedly all the time, and George loses himself in day dreams. In this way, every member adds a certain colour to everyday life. Everyone decides subjectively and spontaneously which colour goes with which group member, by using a paint brush and paints in order to transform all members into blobs on paper.

In a concluding painting round, the artists give reasons for their choice of colour; label the blobs with corresponding first names, and complete the pictures with one or two attributes that explain the nature of the blob a little further.

Materials: paper, paints (for example, water colours), paint brushes

14 The Jumping Worm

All players lie on the floor in such a way that everyone's head lies on the stomach of their predecessor. Using the diaphragm, the first member of the chain worm sends a little jump to the head of the person who is resting on his stomach. As soon as he feels the jump, he creates a diaphragm jump for the next player, and so on.

Tip: A particularly funny variation is the laughing worm. Instead of the sober diaphragm jumps, a happy laugh is passed on, until the whole group is rolling around the floor with laughter.

(15) Guessing Ghosts

This touching game requires a spare bed sheet. The sheet is put over one group member, who then sits down on the floor. Telltale shoes also have to be covered totally by the sheet, because now the guessing begins. Three players who have been waiting outside the door are called in and have to find out through gentle touching who is hidden under the fabric.

Materials: bed sheet

16   **Happy List**

As a rule, unpleasant things are more noticeable than pleasant ones. There also seem to be *more* of the unpleasant things, judging by how often we could get annoyed in a single day …

Now this is brought to the test. Are there really so many less pleasant events, or might it be a matter of how we actually perceive things? An example may make this clearer:

> The pessimist says: 'Oh, dear, the glass is already half empty!'
> The optimist says: 'Great, the glass is still half full!'

Without a doubt, the optimist gets more out of his drink, and probably also more out of a whole day. That is why, from today, a 'happy list' is started. Each group member has their own list. In this any events during the day that triggered a little anger or a lot of fury should be looked at closely. Maybe the event had something good in it after all? How could the emotionally loaded judgement be expressed differently – that is, positively? It is actually not very easy to self-educate for happiness. However, the more practised the eye becomes, the more likely it is to acknowledge: 'This is not worth being angry about, because everything has at least two sides!' An exchange within the group about experiences with the 'happy lists' and observed progress can contribute to positive perceptions.

Materials: paper, pens

17 Group Calendar

In this calendar, there are additional columns next to the column for each day: exactly as many as there are members in the group. That is where everyone enters the time for their own appointments that are not changeable. Plans and commitments that have to be fitted in long term are also considered to be confirmed appointments.

This enables the group to see at a glance where there is room for planning joint activities. Also, the calendar provides information for every group member about who might be under particular pressure at any given time so that, with a little practice and a watchful eye, members can soon work out why another group member is sensitive at a certain time.

Materials: weekly calendar, pens

18 Tick-Tock-Tick

A game for sensitive listeners!

All participants retire to a darkened room. There they find themselves a suitable space, and make themselves comfortable. From now on, eyes must remain closed!

All but one of the players cover their ears. This player hides an alarm clock somewhere in the room. Then that player shouts, 'Tick-tock'. Now the resting participants uncover their ears and concentrate on the sounds. Who can first identify the location of the alarm clock? Anyone who thinks they know makes their guess precisely (for example, 'in the corner behind the piano'). The player who gets closest to the actual hiding place of the alarm clock is allowed to find a new hiding place, and the game moves into the second round.

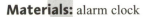

Materials: alarm clock

19 Simply Animals

Each group member is given paper and pens, and then the following instructions are read out:

> Imagine you are an animal.
> Imagine the person next to you is an animal.
> Imagine our whole group are animals.
> Which animal would best suit which person?
>
> Draw our group as an animal family, and label each individual animal with the name of a group member.

All players set to work, making sure they do not forget a single person in the group. Even absent people are included. In a concluding discussion, the artists give reasons for their choice of animals. For example: Tim, a shark – who would have thought that?

A shark is an unpredictable, strong animal. The group now has to discuss together why Ben painted Tim as a shark, and what that could have to do with himself. This can be quite exciting because, when looking at another animal family, one might find Tim as a rabbit, a tiny rabbit who could not hurt a fly.

Materials: paper, pens

20 Contact Sticker

A cork pin-board is required for this activity, as well as pins and a photograph of each participant.

As an introduction to the game, the photo of one group member is pinned in the middle of the board. Now the remaining players position their own photos at a distance from, or proximity to, the starting picture that approximately reflects their real relationship to that group member. At the same time, reasons can be analysed to determine why the 'pictorial' distance has turned out in a particular way. On another day, the next participant is moved to the centre. Who joins them? Who appears to keep more of a distance, and why?

Even when all players have found their social location within the group using this visual method, the diagram is not fixed, because everyone is allowed to change the position of their photo according to the way they feel, and depending on the quantity and quality of their social contacts. The forming of cliques, new friendships, or even rigid 'best friends' becomes apparent.

Tip: At first glance, it may seem a bit much if one person is left standing totally on their own. However, a social structure that has been brought out into the open in this way contains amazing possibilities both for the loner and for the other members of the group. Without a doubt, the person will, on their own, realise that they need to try a little bit harder, and the rest of the group can no longer ignore the fact that there is someone who needs help.

Materials: pin-board, pins, photos of participants

Aggression Games

This section deals with feelings that critically determine the dynamic of a group process: feelings of aggression. The term 'aggression' may conjure up images of loud screaming; physical attacks, threats, and so on. Of course, this open form of aggressive behaviour requires quick intervention in the immediate situation, in order to reach a solution. However, the question arises whether such escalatations could be prevented if you were allowed to get to know aggressions as a permitted part of the individual and by allowing aggressive impulses and actually picking them out as a central theme. Group members may then be able to deal better with negative emotions in the long term.

Just as damaging to the social climate are those hidden feelings of aggression that cannot be recognised at first, and maybe not even at second sight. For example, when well-behaved Henry seemingly rushes to the rescue of chaotic Peter just when everyone can hear – how embarrassing! What did well-behaved Henry get out of it? His small, weaker self is satisfied because, once again, Peter is made to look stupid. The person who should now become angry is, of course, Peter. But he may already have been cast into the role of a loser so often that he may not dare to protest. He suppresses his aggressive feelings; withdraws more and more, and develops a depressive attitude. However, by doing this, he is actually directing the aggression at himself.

However you look at it, feelings of aggression exist and will always be there, in one form or another; but the importance of a healthy potential for aggression is shown in the way people cope with life. To be able to approach one's environment positively; to be able to 'attack' problems, and to participate actively in contacts with others requires a degree of aggressive ability, aimed in a positive and constructive manner.

The following games should help to give the niggling anger in one's stomach a name; to become more aware of negative energies, and so decrease feelings of guilt.

21 Argument Report

The biggest problem in controversial conversations is the fact that the conversational partners concerned do not listen properly to each other. For example, someone may hear a particular word that he does not like at all, and immediately reacts aggressively. Yet he has not actually processed properly the sentence in which the word was embedded – hc has probably not even heard the whole sentence.

In such cases, an argument report can be very useful. Immediately after or during an unexpected argument, all conversational participants sit around a table. Each notes down a kind of 'script' about the preceding scene. For example:

Anna: Tell me, where did my sun-hat end up? The one that Sally took swimming yesterday?
Sally: What? Me? I put the hat on the shelf last night. That is so mean! I am supposed to have lost that stupid hat …

Now both statements are read out carefully and completely. Now repeat each statement shortened to its core content. For example:

Anna: I am looking for my sun-hat.
Sally: I have not used it since yesterday.

Looked at like this, there was actually no real reason for an argument. Wrongly, Sally felt accused simply because she heard her name mentioned in relation to the hat. And, of course, it is not what you say, but the way that you say it.

Materials: paper, pens

22 Compositions in Hate Major

When someone really lets off steam verbally, this is recognisable by the tone and volume of the voice alone.

In a partner game, two players reproduce the rhythmical quality, the tone colour and the volume of such a hate tirade, but without speaking. In other words, the argument melody is translated into a melody made up of humming, grunting and deep throat sounds, in corresponding variable pitch.

In this 'speechless' form, outbursts of rage look particularly ridiculous – maybe even as ridiculous as a real one. The point of extreme fury during arguments should be questioned. The aim of the game is for both partners to compose a moderate argument melody in a question-and-answer style, during which neither of the 'speakers' should be clearly dominant. Both voices should assert themselves alternately, but then should also be able to back off, finishing in a common consent. Alternatively, if no agreement is reached, the voices should break off in a definite but peaceful manner.

Tip: Such a melodic sentence could also be represented graphically, in the form of a diagram.

23 Sock Marbles

We have all experienced being really cross, but only being allowed to let off steam verbally, when we would much rather just punch something really hard! The following game not only allows physical expression, but actually encourages it.

Two players sit opposite each other at a certain distance, and take turns rolling a glass marble to each other. They do this at great speed, so that the thug(s) seated to the side don't know whether they are coming or going. They are each armed with a 'punch sock'. This is a perfectly normal sock, into which another has been stuffed. The 'thugs' wait until the marble whizzes past, and try to give it a good whack. One 'anger point' is given per hit. Good hunting!

Tip: If several sock thugs sit alongside the marble track, they swap places after every five marbles, according to the fairness principle.

Materials: glass marble, socks

24 Pictures of Frustration in Ice

This is a game for the coldest time of the year! Even with sunshine and a blanket of snow, sometime between November and February, we begin to feel a bit claustrophobic. It is in the long, cold months that the human need for activity and festivity is unfulfilled. This is a certain source of aggressive feelings and, thus, a good opportunity to create ice pictures outside.

Each participant requires an empty 'squirty' bottle – for example, a clean washing-up liquid bottle. The bottles are filled with coloured water (water colours, thinned finger paints or food colouring).

Equipped with a good supply of different colours, the group heads off outside. First, a stick is used to mark off a huge picture frame in the snow. Into this frame everyone is allowed to spray an abstract motif or pattern. There are no rules or models. It goes without saying that artists are allowed to swap colours among themselves. The game is finished when every player has immortalised themselves in the snow picture with every desired colour.

Afterwards, you could have a grand opening with hot punch and torchlight!

Materials: squirty bottles, colours (water colours, finger paints)

---

(25) Washing Each Other's Heads

This German saying implies that we would really like to tell someone else what we think of them, exorcising their fantasies or simply 'washing off' their wrong attitudes.

So why not introduce a ritual that involves an annoyed group member washing the head of the person who represents the cause of their anger? This could involve a conventional hair wash, or a scalp massage with some nice hair lotion or simply miming the action. During this pleasurable procedure, the 'coiffeur' is allowed to air verbally their accumulated anger in an appropriate form. They are allowed to let off steam for as long as it takes to carry out the hair wash. The person who is being 'washed' is allowed only to listen quietly – and to enjoy!

When having such pleasant treatment, it is easier to swallow even harsh criticism. And all worries are swept away down the drain when the hair is being rinsed.

Materials: water, shampoo

26 Angry Salt Faces

A salt dough is made from 300g flour, 300g salt, and water. While kneading the dough, participants can 'let off steam'. As soon as the dough ceases to be sticky and comes away easily from the bowl, the participants turn to the creative part.

Following the theme 'I am so cross', participants are allowed to design really horrible angry faces – creepy, grotesque faces which, once they have been dried at 150°C (300°F, Gas mark 2) in the oven, are painted in bright colours.

Even if the place might temporarily look like a ghost train, it does not matter, because the anger was recognised before being banished to the wall.

Materials: flour, salt, water, paints (for example, poster paint)

27 Special Vocabulary Book for Inventors

Throwing verbal abuse at each other is not really difficult, especially when this involves the most basic swearwords which, today, have been mastered even by toddlers. But what happens when group members are asked to 'swear' intelligently: when they have to look for new, creative word inventions or sayings with class? While they are supposed to express criticism and anger, they are not allowed to be offensive. The ability of group members to master the art of rhetoric can be determined by reading individual group members' special vocabulary books. This is where everyone can record their ideas and word creations, in anger but legibly.

At the end of the month, for example, a happy round of intelligent swearing can take place.

> Hollow-sounding watering can!
>
> Grim nutcracker!

Materials: paper, pens

28 **Soft Ball**

Instead of giving someone an outdated and inappropriate caning on their bottom, this game involves using the same target, but also laughing as much as possible.

All participants – angry or not – stand in a line and rest their hands on their upper thighs. Behind them, at a distance of about 3 metres, stands the first 'hunter', armed with a very soft ball. At a given signal he tries to hit each of the lined-up players on the bottom, scoring one point per hit. It is even better if he can also explain why the person opposite deserved the smack on the bottom!

Materials: soft ball

(29) Balloon Attack

A circle is marked out on the floor, using a long scarf or string. The circle represents a nest for one player who has to look after an inflated balloon. The 'defender' protects the 'egg' by covering it with their upper body. Then the signal to start is given and an attacker goes after the air-filled booty. They have to try to burst the balloon by pinching or squashing it, or they may try to put pressure on the balloon by, for example, lying on top of the defender.

Rule 1: The use of sharp objects is not allowed!

Rule 2: If the 'egg' falls out of the nest, the fight is temporarily interrupted until the balloon has been retrieved.

Materials: scarves or string, balloons

30 The Tearing Party

Before the game begins, every player recalls when they last felt anger – especially anger that was never expressed. In other words, anger that is still seething and looking for revenge.

Then participants proceed to action: each grabs a pile of newspapers and, without mercy, rips each page into small pieces. At the end of this frenzied activity – for example, after a kitchen timer goes off – all participants should have exhausted themselves.

All the pieces of paper are put in a bucket filled with glue, and are well mashed up. Reconciliation then takes place. On a large piece of paper or card, everyone builds a lumpy piece of art from the pulp – a mountain maybe, that expresses the size of the frustrations experienced, which the players have now finally finished with. When the 'memorial' has dried off, the now pacified participants are allowed to decorate it with paint, as a memento for an unforgettable tearing party.

Materials: one old newspaper per participant, a tub of wallpaper glue, a large sheet of strong paper or cardboard

31 Attention, Tantrum

Here, an emergency is anticipated and humorously commented upon. Participants are asked to describe signs, first-aid measures, and so on to treat an outbreak of anger.

The group puts together the text as teamwork, writing on a large sheet of paper. The completed poster is given a place of honour somewhere in the room, so that it only needs to be pointed at when a row flares up between any of the participants. For example:

Signs
The person's face becomes a red to purple colour.
He shouts louder than a howling monkey.
His eyes stick out.
He gasps for air.
He clenches his fists.

First aid
Put him in the recovery position.
Put a plaster over his lips.
Pass him a cloth to wipe the sweat away.

Counter-measures
Whispering to the angry person.
Making legitimate compliments.
Covering one's mouth to indicate that tantrums are boring.

Materials: large sheet of paper, pens

Liberating Dances

When there is a bad atmosphere, playing the right music can work wonders. Group members are allowed to take it in turns to bring in their favourite music tapes, which are used when required. Regardless of location (for example, in the room, in the gym or outside) participants dance around freely, without any particular rhythm or movement being insisted upon. It is even better if the group leader also breaks into ecstatic twitches! Physical and emotional letting-go is not actually that easy; only when there is no embarrassment can relaxation through liberating dances be guaranteed.

Materials: cassettes, CDs, cassette/CD player

(33) The Grumpy Frog

One player sits in the middle of the circle. He has the task of responding to all questions addressed to him by the players sitting around him with a sulky and cross 'No' while trying not to laugh. 'Do you want a lolly?' 'No!' shouts the grumpy frog, angrily looking around the circle. 'Would you like to go deep-sea diving with Flipper?' 'Do you fancy a burger?' And so on. The questions become funnier and funnier and, in addition, those asking the questions try to use speech and gestures that will really test the frog.

With players grimacing and making funny noises, how can the grumpy frog remain sulky? The aim is achieved when the grumpy frog cannot help but grin. He is then allowed to choose the next miserable person, who now has to put the strength of his composure to the test.

34 Cat and Mouse

The following drawing game serves to uncover possible latent feelings of aggression. All players have at least two sheets of paper and a pen. The leader asks two questions, one after the other. The first question is: 'Which big, strong animal comes to your mind first? Draw it quickly.' The second question is: 'Which little, weak animal comes to mind first? Draw it on the same piece of paper.'

The leader now moves on to the creative phase with a short story: 'You have drawn two animals: a big one and a little one. Imagine that these animals – even though this might sound unlikely – meet in the jungle by the side of a river. What happens? Draw a story of what you think might happen.'

Note: Participants should set to work immediately, without any preceding discussion. Some kind of screen would also be useful in order to achieve truly individual results.

Tip: Exaggerated scenes of friendship between the two animals, or extreme helpfulness in the story, can also indicate aggression: for example, when the artist concerned is not actually very successful with that sort of friendship in real life. A subsequent discussion of the pictures can throw up information about this.

Materials: paper, pens

(35) Lemon Duel

Two duellers stand facing each other. Each holds in one hand a tablespoon on which there is a lemon. The fight starts: seconds out for the first lemon duel!

The duellers approach each other and try to knock the other's lemon off the spoon. At the same time they protect themselves from attack with their free arm. The duellist whose fruit lands on the floor first has lost the round. As a consolation, the winner passes over a thin slice of lemon, which the loser bravely sucks: a vitamin blast which will strengthen them for further rounds!

Materials: tablespoons, lemons

36 Wham, Bang, Alakazam

The leader gets hold of some paper bags, for example from a bakery – one for each participant.

All players sit in a circle and blow up their bags. The bag opening is scrunched together, so that the air cannot escape prematurely. Everyone now raises their free hand to get ready for the bang. Players remain in this pose until it is their turn. The first player smacks their bag and, as soon as the bang has died away, the person next to them carries on, bang; this second noise is the signal for the third player, and so on. In this way, a banging develops around the circle. Yet, at the same time, a common interest is involved, because every player must wait their turn, one after the other, and so the optimal wham, bang, alakazam chain is created.

Materials: paper bags

(37) Pushing About

A large blanket is spread out on the floor. Then each player finds a partner of equal size. Now the pushing about begins! The players put their hands together and try to push each other off the blanket area. After the first round with hand contact, a second trial takes place shoulder to shoulder. Other possibilities are bottom to bottom, tummy to tummy, and head to head. *With the last variation, however, a thick cushion should be used as a buffer.*

A round has finished as soon as one of the pushers has both feet outside the blanket area.

Materials: blanket

38 Attack of the Wolves

Players draw lots to become wild wolves or tame sheep. Large sticky labels (as many as there are players) are marked with symbols: for example, a red tooth for the wolf, a yellow circle for the woolly sheep. There are as many wolves as there are sheep.

Everyone reaches into the bag and chooses a label. Another player sticks the label on to the person's back.

Now the sheep start moving around innocently. They try to portray the characters of the sheep through body posture and movement: rather hesitant, taking small steps, fearful, clumsy, needing loving care, and so on.

As soon as the signal is given, the attack of the wolves takes place. Powerful, and with supple grace, they hunt their victims; they show their teeth; growl; howl, and threaten – yet without actually touching any of the sheep. At an opportune moment both animal groups are allowed to pull the label off the back of an animal from the other group. As soon as this has happened, the two players swap animals. Otherwise, a role reversal is announced after five minutes.

Materials: sticky labels, pens

39 Elastic Jail

Elastic jail is a great skill game for budding Houdinis – and little thugs also get their money's worth!

In each round, a maximum of two to three players are in action. Each group also requires some elastic, approximately 4 metres long, with the ends tied together. And that is all it takes.

One player remains passive, standing absolutely still in the middle, and lets their partner wrap them up as skilfully as possible. The third player stands to the side. They can help, for example, to pull the elastic over the passive player's head, around an ankle and from there back up to the shoulder, and so on. In addition, it is their job to make sure that the person who is being tied up is not hurt (*wrapping the elastic around the neck is strictly forbidden*).

As soon as the last centimetre of the elastic has been used, the tied-up player is allowed to get to work. With fingertips and skilfulness they are likely to manage to get out of the elastic jail. It is just a matter of not getting impatient!

Materials: elastic

40 Skittles

Let's be honest: don't we all sometimes feel the urge to grab another person by the collar, to shake them, or to 'knock them over'?

For this purpose, pasta tubes (uncooked) are labelled with the names of group members, or have faces painted on them. These 'people' are now lined up at the end of a long table. At the opposite end, the first sportsman or sportswoman is waiting. Armed with a glass marble, they try their luck. Using an underarm movement, they take aim and roll the 'bowl' towards their comrades. They have two goes. Do they manage to knock over all their pasta friends? The number of hits is counted and noted down. The winner is the person with the most points. To celebrate, they could be allowed to prepare a pasta sauce to make a tasty dish for everyone.

Materials: pasta tubes, pens, marbles

Reconciliation & Rest Games

There should be as many reconciliations as there are conflicts that have to be survived and put up with in the group. It is the forgiving actually facilitates constructive arguing. People cannot learn to stand up energetically for their opinion when they have experienced, as a consequence, the affection of others being withdrawn; in other words, loss of love being used as a punishment for initiative. Children and young people in particular are dependent on signs of reconciliation; but grown-ups, too, require such calming feedback after controversial exchanges, in order to move freely within the group afterwards – even when they would prefer to think that they are above such things.

Reconciliation can be offered directly, verbally, which itself requires high social competence, or games can be used, which inevitably bring people closer to each other. During a game, often there need only be an exchanged glance, smile or a little physical contact to melt the ice.

In today's bustle and hectic rush, we frequently lack the time to care properly for interpersonal relationships. Often, new events are planned; one appointment closely follows another; we wait impatiently for a special party, and so on. Within this 'and-what-comes-next?' attitude, we overlook the need for rest and quietness; where past experiences can continue to have an effect; where emotional needs are allowed to surface; where the yearning for harmony and closeness has a place.

41 The Baby Wants to Sleep

The following rest game is particularly suitable as a conclusion to a lively day, but it may be used simply as a means to establish quiet at any time.

In the middle of the room lies a player, all snuggled up on a soft and comfortable cushion. He represents the baby that has just fallen asleep. Somewhere in the room there are nosy visitors, who want to admire the sleeping infant. One after the other they tiptoe as quietly as possible in the direction of the cot. As soon as the infant hears even the tiniest sound he gives off a baby-like squeal and points his hand in the direction from which, in his opinion, the sound has come. As a result, the clumsy visitor concerned has to return to his original place, and another player tries his luck. Anyone who manages to get right up to the baby without making a sound is allowed to stroke the baby's hair gently three times. Afterwards, a role reversal takes place, and the successful visitor makes himself comfortable in the cot. He is the sleepy baby for the next round.

Materials: cushion or soft base

42 Dream Swings

In Native American medicine, dreams are assigned a lot of meaning. Even small children are encouraged to remember their dreams, to 'work' with them. Because many things are covered up in everyday living – decisions that are being put off, and fears that no one is allowed to see – all these things come to the surface in dreams, and can even help the dreamer to find the right solution.

The group gets together to 'dream swing'. In a room lit by candles, it is wonderfully easy to talk of the night when the monster grabbed all the exercise books; or of the brilliant dream when you sailed through the jungle on a sailing ship; or of the dream that you have every night – always the same one – that wakes you up startled every time, and that you would rather not ever dream again. Through this dream work, which is really exciting and comforting, but which also leads to discovery, an atmosphere of special trust can develop, where one can get to know other group members, as well as oneself, even better.

Materials: candles

43 A Note to Help Carol Remember

Carol is always helpful, and is always ready to listen to any group member. Her hobbies are cooking and handicrafts. Everyone likes Carol, but because Carol is great, so brilliant and natural that no one ever gives her another thought.

For this Carol (or Carl) who, in some shape or form, exists in every group, a note is filed in a notebook: 'Thank you to Carol.' The note is supposed to remind everyone that it is really important to see and recognise the achievements of others. Every quiet helper will be pleased at such little gestures, and then helping becomes twice as much fun.

Materials: Post-it note, or small piece of paper

44 Smelly Clothes

Apparently, the quality of an interpersonal relationship is determined by how well individuals can stand the smell of each other. The following game is supposed to prove the extent to which everyone actually has this ability! Each group member wears a little scarf around his neck for a day. The scarf must not be visible to anyone else. The best thing to do is to hide it under a roll-neck jumper.

In the evening of the same day, everyone is called for the clothes-smelling competition. All players discreetly put their little scarf into a pot. This scarf pot is then put in the middle of the circle. One after the other, players take out a scarf (of course, not their own), and carry out a conscientious smell test. Well? Are they going to be able to name the wearer of the scarf? Any statement along the lines of, 'This one stinks' should be deliberately ignored, while players with a 'good nose' are rewarded with 100 'smelly points'.

Materials: one small scarf per player, a pot or similar container

(45) Touching Chain

The group is seated in a circle on the floor. The person to begin – a different person every time – thinks of a special part of the face that they want to gently touch. The tip of the nose, perhaps? They start with that player to whom they currently feel emotionally closest, and touch them gently on the nose. The touched player immediately passes on this proof of friendship in the same way (same place, same strength, courageously or timidly, and so on) to their neighbour.

Tip: Sons and daughters who are going through puberty should not be excused from this game. Often especially stubborn teenagers have a particular need for a tender gesture, and the power of habit eventually takes away the fear of touch.

46 Three Wishes

A fairy tale game! Each participant closes their eyes and quietly lets their most secret and greatest wishes pass in front of their minds' eye, without any censorship. Afterwards, players are allowed to paint or draw their wishes on to a single large piece of paper. Calming background music is played at the same time.

Each player is given as much time as he needs. Looking at, and talking about, the pictures afterwards will provide some information regarding why individual group members may not feel all that comfortable in their current role. Of course, this game cannot change basic conditions. Nevertheless, the opportunity to be heard and, most of all, to be allowed the spiritual freedom to dream, strengthens trust in the rest of the group tremendously.

Materials: paper, pens

(47) The Treasure in the Fridge

'The way to a man's heart is through his stomach': this saying is only too true! For this reason, it makes sense to fill the fridge in the common room for use after a particularly 'hairy' situation. This could involve a popular pudding in a large bowl, or it could be a platter (to be eaten in the ancient Roman manner: lying on the floor using fingers), or maybe a selection of colourfully decorated hard-boiled eggs (not just at Easter time). There are no limits to group members' imagination.

Someone can introduce the reconciliation meal with a saying made up by the group:

'We are all happy!
We all like each other a lot!
Everyone eats as much as they can,
be they woman or man – dig in!'

Materials: anything that tastes good

48 **Concept of Harmony**

The group's task is to draw up a joint 'concept of harmony', in the form of a poem or a piece of prose, on a large sheet of paper. The poster is to be put up on the wall in a prominent place, so that it can be looked at daily, and remind group members of positive intentions that will facilitate a harmonious social atmosphere.

What do we like; what gives us pleasure; what are the requirements for an atmosphere of trust, and so on? After a discussion of ideas for living together, the group sets to work. The literary outpourings of the individual group members are collected first, and these are then integrated into a complete piece of art. For example:

> Happiness in the morning
> gets rid of all sorrow.
> A friend who means you well
> says, 'Hi'.
> Tolerance towards everyone,
> that's what we would like ...
> If someone is crying,
> put your arm around them.
> That makes it easier,
> a smile keeps you warm.

Materials: sheet of paper (poster), pens

49 The Peace Cocktail

The peace cocktail is to group members what the peace pipe is to Native Americans.

For this, all participants who are ready for a reconciliation sit around a table. In the middle of the table there are a selection of different drinks: several different types of juice, lemonade, mineral water, tonic water, and small pieces of cut-up fruit or herbs. Each cocktail mixer has one or two empty glasses in front of him, in which he mixes the most unusual creations.

In the end, the group votes on the taste that comes closest to a peace cocktail. Then every player takes a drink from that cocktail using his straw. And, just as with Native Americans, the argument is now forgotten, buried and drowned. Cheers!

Materials: different types of drink, fruit, glasses, straws

50 In the Mask

This game allows group members to rid themselves of any fear of physical contact, because they are having make-up put on. A sketch is made by the painters before they put on the make-up. Particularly unsociable players can 'cling' to this as a kind of distraction while they are painting their partner.

Having to copy the sketch makes it easier to put cream gently on to the skin of the person opposite, then to add paint and powder. Finally, the finished masks are given awards according to how much care went into the work, which required sensitivity, endurance, and a certain amount of affection during the contact.

Tip: Don't forget your camera!

Materials: make-up utensils, face paints, a camera

(51) Chinese Humming

'Chinese humming' is the wordless variation of Chinese whispers, where the first person whispers a secret word or message into the ear of their neighbour. This time, though, players do not whisper, but hum.

The message should be a friendly rather than a grumpy one, expressed through the tune, and more of a light sound, a soft expression. The first player passes the hummed message to their neighbour; they copy it into the ear of their neighbour, and so on. It remains to be heard what melody is going to arrive with the last player in the chain. Can they decode the message?

'I like you' could have been the initial message, but saying it is not actually that easy. However, with a bit of practice, maybe even 'spoken hummed messages' can be sent; who knows?

52) The Reconciliation Cake

A simple Madeira-type cake is baked by the group in the kitchen. If this is too much work, a cake can be bought. The most important thing about the reconciliation cake, however, is its decoration. For this one needs enough icing in the desired colour or flavour. In addition, everyone joining in the meal is required to bring something small that can be pressed into the icing. A sort of 'reconciliation pledge' that will be kept secret until the icing is beginning to set. Quickly, participants stick on their mini-surprise, and the beauty of the cake is complete. Well, if that is not an occasion for a little harmonious teatime …

Variation: There is also the option of a reconciliation flag cake. Here, everyone sticks a small piece of paper or a jam label on to a toothpick, and sticks the decorated labelled flag on to the finished cake.

Materials: cake, icing, different edible mini-surprises (for example, jelly babies)

53 A Guessing Massage

Regardless of whether the selected participant is a headstrong person acutely at risk of bickering, or a persistent grouch, today he will receive the special pleasure of a guessing massage.

For this, the player lies on his stomach or side on the floor. A towel or a small pillow should make lying down more comfortable. Then he is covered with a fluffy blanket and is allowed to close his eyes. From now on, peeping is not allowed! The first masseur creeps up on tiptoe, and begins to massage the person through the blanket: calm, circular movements, rhythmical tapping movements, up-and-down massaging, and so on. In so doing, they write their initial on the back of the passive player, as large as possible and across the whole of their back. Is the 'sleeper' going to recognise their benefactor? In any case, this gives them a reason for putting up with the 'childish' massage: after all, they must guess the correct answer – and being massaged is simply wonderful, even for cool boys (of all ages).

Materials: cushion, soft base, blanket

54 Fingers in the Feely Bag

A cardboard box is filled with rice, dried lentils and peas. Three to four players each sink one hand into the box and with relish dig around in the corn heap – a fantastic feeling for every single finger! The same players now go in search of other fingers. One may spontaneously jerk back, or find the unexpected touch 'super-funny'. In any case, players continue touching and searching until everyone knows whose hand they are holding at a particular moment.

Tip 1: A cloth is put over all submerged hands to make the game even more exciting.

Tip 2: Foot guessing, too, can be good fun.

Materials: cardboard box, rice, lentils, peas

55 'If I were you ...'

Each player begins his speech with these words. All the players are seated in a circle. The person who begins has a little stick with which he quickly points to another player about whom he can remember something, saying, for example, 'If I were you, I wouldn't overdo your sports training.' The person who is being addressed simply acknowledges the message by nodding, then snatches up the stick, points it in the direction of another player, and puts themselves in their shoes: 'If I were you, I would look for different friends', or 'If I were you, I would try to develop my musical talent.'

Rule: Judgemental words such as good or bad should, if possible, be avoided. Anyone who feels offended can drop out.

Tip: This very honest and open game should be discussed beforehand. The purpose of the game is to approach another group member objectively and spontaneously, and to give them a hint in a non-judgemental and decent way, or maybe hold up a critical mirror to them.

This game requires a trusting atmosphere.

Materials: small stick

56 Table Mail

Today, a light, plain-coloured, disposable table cloth covers the group table. Every player holds a pen and thinks of a reconciliation message, or a small declaration of friendship. They then dress it up in nice words and write it on the outer edge of the table cloth. Then everyone sitting around the table closes their eyes and, at a command, they turn the table cloth – Heave-ho, heave-ho, heave-ho – until someone shouts 'Stop!' Everyone opens their eyes and reads what is written in front of them.

Whether kissy-bear has hit on the correct receiver remains an open question. In any case, the 'wrong' receiver will also be pleased by such funny table mail.

Materials: disposable table cloth, pens

(57) The Mascot

A large piece of paper, positioned so that it is longer than it is wide, is drawn on by the first player, who draws some form of headgear right at the top. The hat, cap, or hair is folded over and the piece of paper is passed to the next player, who invents a face for the group mascot. Again, this is folded over, and passed to the third person, who does the neck part, including the shirt collar; the next player creates clothes for the upper body, and so on, until, in the end, a funny person is the result. The mascot thus created is outlined with a black felt-tip pen and coloured in.

Materials: paper, pens

58 Here's Looking at You, Kid

Everyone knows this saying. In the style of Humphrey Bogart, this game is about seeing whether a person can look another group member in the eye, and for how long, because this is actually a really tricky and difficult task.

Two participants sit opposite each other. Without an external signal, the two decide for themselves when they are ready to start. Some people might prefer to carry out this exercise without spectators.

Everyone should try the game with each of the other group members at some point.

Without passing much judgement, participants are allowed to acknowledge the course of the looking games. Whether the person who looked away first was the weaker or more sensitive person, or whether the person with the strong look is the stronger one remains an open question.

It is important afterwards to think about the personality of the person opposite; to sense what sort of person they have been looking in the eye; and to think about what they have found out about themselves.

(59) Heart is Trumps

On the pavement, the heart of a player is drawn with chalk. It is, for example, Oscar's heart. The name written in the centre of the drawing.

All group members get hold of a good number of small pebbles, and line up behind a throwing line. The aim of the game is to land as many stones as possible in Oscar's heart. It is a great feeling when, once in a while, all your friends can be really close to your heart …

Materials: chalk, small pebbles

60 Taking a Deep Breath

Deliberate breathing is an excellent way to calm oneself down. The following relaxation exercise can be carried out even with small children. For them, the exercise can be called the '1-2-3 puffing game'.

All participants sit comfortably on their chairs. As an introduction, everyone is asked to breathe in deeply, and then breathe out, or sing out, as loudly as possible, a few times, which may sound a bit like a siren. They begin with the highest note possible and end very low. Breathing out follows a definite and individually chosen letter sequence, for example 'pfoo', 'hia', 'hi', 'miaow' and so on. (Vowels in initial position are not recommended, because they easily prompt pushing.)

This choir of sirens sounds very funny, and makes players laugh. That is great, because it makes the second, more serious, part of the exercise easier. Here each participant puts both hands on their stomach. They now breathe in against the weight of their hands, with the stomach bulging out. While doing this, everyone slowly counts to three to themselves, and then lets the air stream out again, while again counting to three. This breathing exercise is repeated until a feeling of relaxation has been established.

Tip: Let anyone who wants to carry out the exercise lying down. Don't forget some sort of soft surface, such as a blanket, to lie on.

Materials: blanket

Autonomy Games

The quality of social relationships is immediately dependent on the power structure existing within a group. Are there certain people who tend always to have their say, and who thus restrict other group members or even oppress them? Or are there particularly weak people who use their inability and their weakness (deliberately or subconsciously) to put other group members at their service? Are there inconspicuous and calm group members who maybe work away busily, but never show themselves to advantage in a social context, and who thus strengthen the feeling of power of the strong members even further?

It is obvious that the power structure tends to be most unbalanced where there are young or very young people who belong to a group or join a group as newcomers. They require help, and run the biggest danger of being completely controlled.

The foundations for self-confidence and independence are laid during infancy. So, if we can give children the feeling that they are beings to be taken seriously; give them a secure place with freedom for creative development, and allow them to learn sufficiently to become themselves, we will have made important steps towards the development of a positive overall climate. 'Satisfaction' is the key word here. If every person experiences themselves as welcome – as important and competent – they will be satisfied with themselves. And with that satisfaction, the desire for voluntary and constructive togetherness increases.

A requirement for the development of autonomy is the feeling of being accepted, and of belonging to a group community. Safety and security provide the courage for individual development. Further, it is important to grant every person the right to their own opinion, and to seriously ask in what respects, in their opinion, this person might be right (even if their opinion does not reflect that of the group). An unreflected 'no' should also sometimes be accepted as valid, because only someone who has learned to say 'no' will also be able openly to say 'yes' to something.

Also people – especially those who have just joined a group – should experience being allowed to act individually, too. Perhaps a corner of the room may be reserved for individual activities.

Looking at results, ideas and social achievements together as a group, as well as evaluating things individually, have a lot of value. This does not mean the exaggerated glorification of individuals, which would only lead to jealousy. The fast sprinter welcomes recognition of his running times just as much as, for example, the poet for his eloquent use of language, or the handyman for his clever alteration of the hamster cage into a handcart.

The development of autonomy also requires opportunities for creating distance while being close. The fact that, sometimes, someone simply wants to be left alone in order to be able to approach others with renewed strength later on should be respected.

And finally, it is important to experience one's own limitations; to learn to cope with times of frustration, and to be able to cope when things do not go according to plan.

This section includes 20 games to strengthen a self-confident attitude in children, to signal to them that they are important.

(61) Here Lives ...

When a group of people live behind a closed door, no one actually knows who it is that can be found behind that door. That is why a large door sign should be made, containing the names of all group members, even the youngest. After all, everyone is important: even the young, it is hoped, know this already. And to make really sure that no one is being overlooked, you could add something else under the door sign: for example, a coloured strip of cardboard on which every group member prints their footprint, to show that everyone here is on an equal footing!

Materials: cardboard, coloured pens, finger paints

62 Today is Decision Day

All group members write their names on a piece of paper. The pieces of paper are folded and put in a pot. Then they are drawn in turn. The names are noted down in the order of drawing, and given numbers. The player who has been drawn first is 'Decision-Maker 1'. Players are allowed to choose a day where they have the say for three hours: which games are going to be played; who should be invited; which songs are going to be sung – all this is determined by 'Decision-Maker 1' during the agreed time.

'Decision-Maker 2' enjoys the same privileges on another day; 'Decision-Maker 3' chooses another date for his autocratic rule, and so on. What fun, no one else is allowed to interfere. Hopefully the person responsible can come up with a full and comprehensive programme.

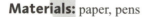

Materials: paper, pens

63 Tina Burger and Nina Noodle

Everyone has a favourite meal. For example, Tina's mouth starts watering at the thought of fish-burgers. However, there have to be exactly two fish fingers and a radish between two bread roll halves, smothered with tomato sauce and mayonnaise. Nina loves curly noodles with cheese sauce, and a blob of jam on top. Tastes differ, after all. But it is great when one's own name is directly associated with such a yummy delicacy. It makes an impression if even a meal 'has been named after me'. Bon appetit!

Tip: Such special meals can also be named after whole groups or families.

Materials: anything that tastes nice

64 A Name Like One Out of a Picture Book

Does this sound familiar? A child comes to school. The child is asked what his name is. The child answers: 'Sweetie Smith'. To spare the child embarrassment, one has to be aware of his real first name, and always use it when addressing the child. A name can play an important part in defining a person's identity.

The following game is about creatively decorating and arranging one's own first name. Each player – it is especially important not to omit the younger ones in a group – is given a strip of paper and a coloured pen. In large capital letters and with plenty of distance between individual letters, they then write their first name on the strip of paper. An adult takes on this part of the activity for children who cannot yet write their names. Then the fiddly bit starts! A picture needs to be found for every letter of the name (around it, inside it) that fits the shape of a particular letter.

The finished creations are then stuck to the respective doors, or pinned on to a group poster.

Materials: paper, coloured pens

65 **Flower King and Flower Queen**

Flowers are often given the most precious names: lily of the valley, Black-eyed Susan, passion flower, and so on. In this game, every group member is allowed to plant a flower bulb in a pot of earth. The pot is labelled with a sign on which the real name of the planter, as well as an invented fairy-tale name of the flower, is written.

The children then put the pots on the windowsill and tends to the bulb's daily needs.

Important: Ask the children to imagine themselves to be the bulb or flower. What sort of care would they need? What sort of result could be achieved with good care? This can be an exciting game, especially when accompanying group discussions also make the link to the individual. What sort of care would I need myself; what sort of treatment would be good for me; what sort of regular 'tender loving care' would it take to ensure that personal efforts bear fruit in real life?

Tip: Amaryllis bulbs are particularly suitable. They produce several flowers of enormous dimensions.

Materials: flower pots, compost, flower bulbs, paper, pens

66 My Little Me-Bag

A me-bag is a small bag that can hang around the neck of the child. In it are lots of things that are of the utmost importance: things that provide information about the child's identity (in case he gets lost on holiday, in the supermarket, on an outing, for example; a home-made copy of his passport, a card with his address and telephone number, maybe a note with information about his health, such as important medication or allergies). Also in the bag are all those things that the child thinks he cannot do without – for example, a picture of his hamster; an address book with the addresses of his best friends; grandad's lucky marble and, of course, a small purse. Finally, the bag is completed with a whistle and a brightly coloured balloon. These two items can help him in an emergency to attract attention, either by blowing the whistle, or by waving the balloon – 'Hello, I am here!'

The me-bag can also be used effectively in the following cases. When groups go out, they generally plan a couple of meal breaks. However, it becomes a bit of a nuisance if, in addition, there are breaks because someone needs a tissue, or someone else wants to know what address he is supposed to put on his postcard. The me-bag can help to avoid this sort of stress!

Materials: small bag, copy of child's passport, purse, various things

(67) It's Me

This catch game involves recognising group members by their voices.

One player, the catcher, stands facing the wall. The other participants gather around behind him and remain very quiet. Using only gestures, they agree on the next speaker. That player then taps the back of the catcher three times, who, in turn, has to ask: 'Who is that?' The 'tapper' simply responds with the word 'Me!' Does the catcher recognise who has tapped him on the shoulder? If not, he is allowed to ask twice more, but still only gets the same brief answer. As soon as the catcher has called out the correct name of the 'tapper', that person has to run off as quickly as possible, and the catcher runs after him. When the catcher has caught the 'tapper', the 'tapper' becomes the catcher for the second round.

68 **Lion, Bird, Mouse**

For this game, the leader prepares about 10 questions. Each question is written on a separate piece of card, with the answer written in brackets underneath the question. The children do not necessarily have to be able to answer all the questions, but should be encouraged to have a guess, select *one* answer out of a choice of three, and indicate their choice in the form of a 'squiggle'. Funny questions should definitely be given preference!

Then the leader picks a question card and reads out the first question. The children have a piece of paper on which they can see only the three answers with the three squiggle boxes. Each column is assigned an animal symbol. Who is going to be right: the bird, the mouse, or the lion? For example:

What is a baby deer called?	fawn	dawn	yawn
Question 2 …			
Question 3 … and so on.			

The children all participate in the same round and sit in front of *one* piece of paper. They listen to the first question: 'What is a baby deer called?'

The children are given half-a-minute's thinking time before they can check the answer on the question card. Is a baby deer called a fawn, a dawn, or a yawn? The children quickly decide on an answer, and put a squiggle in the appropriate box, without looking at what their neighbours to left and right have written.

Each child uses a different colour for his squiggle. Any correct answer squiggles are highlighted by the leader with a special larger squiggle in a yellow highlighter pen.

This way, you can tell easily at the end who has made the *right decisions* and how often.

Tip 1: During this game, one could think about why Tony and his friend Henry have always put a squiggle in the same (mostly wrong) box. Which of these two does not dare to have his own opinion? Probably the child who put down his squiggle second.

Tip 2: It is possible that some children let themselves be influenced by the picture symbols: a big, strong lion has got to be right, hasn't it?

Materials: paper, pens

(**69**) Largometer Pictures

To be among the youngest and smallest in a group is really unfair. 'Wait until you have grown', they are told. How mean! But what would happen if the group minis were to turn into giants, who seemingly have a lot of influence and a lot of authority?

Nothing could be easier: on a hot summer's day, take the youngest children by the hand, and lead them into the sun. There they throw huge shadows on to the pavement. Quickly get some chalk and start drawing. The outlines of the suddenly-grown child are captured in colour on the pavement, and finally measured with a tape measure.

Tip: Let any child who wants to lay a large strip of paper on the floor, and draw the shadow picture on that – to keep, and as motivation for particularly bad days.

Materials: chalk, measuring tape

70 Contact Traffic Lights

During interpersonal encounters and contacts the question of closeness and distance plays an important role. Often you want to be left in peace, but finding yourself all alone is not nice either. At those times you might like close contact with another person, but that person, of all people, could be in a bad mood: a difficult situation, which is the origin for many self-doubts.

For the following game, each child requires three cardboard circles (approximately 15cm [6"] in diameter) that are coloured in and made to look like traffic lights. The circles are loosely threaded on to a piece of string, so they cannot get lost while the child is walking. Equipped in such a way, players now walk, run and jump around the room. Next, everyone tries to make contact with another participant, by standing in front of one of them in a questioning manner, or by pointing a finger at someone. The person 'addressed' can now react in one of three ways:

◆ If the red traffic light is shown it means 'I want to be left in peace. Please leave me alone.' Both players carry on walking.

◆ The amber traffic light means 'I am not so sure. What is it you want to play?' In response, the person seeking contact has to make a suggestion that the other person can accept or reject in a friendly manner.

◆ The green traffic light signals 'Welcome, I have been waiting for you. Let's go and play together.' The players link arms and walk together for a little while. Then they separate and begin anew to seek contact in the circle of players.

This game sensitises players to the necessary distance from and closeness to others, and sharpens self-perception.

Materials: cardboard circles, coloured pens in red, amber (orange/yellow) and green

71   The Wish Hotel

A large house is drawn on the pavement using chalk. The house has as many windows as there are players. Each player draws a portrait of themselves in one of the windows. Then the game starts. All players find a small pebble, and line up along a chalked line. Pay attention: the first throw counts!

Anyone who throws their pebble into their own window can make a special wish. This could be to be allowed to stay up longer one evening, to be served their favourite meal, or to decide where the next outing is going to be to – it does not matter: anyone who hits their own window can choose.

Rule: Materialistic wishes are taboo!

Materials: chalk, pebbles

(72) Open End

Finding an ending for a story requires the ability to make decisions, as well as the ability to think in a structured way, and to proceed with a plan in mind. It does not matter in this game whether the youngest in the group is able to write, because the story ending should be in picture form anyway.

For this game, the leader chooses a suitable picture book from the library, appropriate to the cognitive level of the group. Particularly appropriate are those picture-book stories that include some sort of climax. With the players sitting in a circle, the book should be shown and discussed (the professional variation would be the use of overheads, or slides of the individual pictures). And what is going to happen next?

Now creativity and courage are asked for because, however strange an individual's idea for the story ending may appear, that idea may not actually be the worst.

Materials: picture book, paper, pens

73 Programme Announcement

The bottom is cut from a cardboard box, leaving a 2 cm [1"] wide border, so creating a new cardboard box television. The players prepare for their presentation. For this they research the television programmes for the day, and look for exciting programmes, documentaries or films that may be of interest to the group. Everyone then chooses a programme, and puts together a short television announcement. The information for this is obtained from a television guide and any ideas that they picked up when they last watched the programme. Guesses as to what a particular film may be about can be made for those films for which there are few details in the guide.

The first presenter then sits behind the cardboard television; greets the viewers; gives reasons for their choice; briefly outlines the programme and then – real television on and the film begins. Did the presenter make a good choice?

Materials: cardboard television, paper with television programmes

(74) Emperor, We Want to Come and See You

This chasing game is a variation of the game 'What's the time, Mr Wolf?' The 'Emperor' stands by the far wall of a large room, or a house if the players are outside. He waves majestically to his people. Then the people call in unison: 'Emperor, we want to come and see you!' The Emperor answers: 'That is not possible!' But his followers are not easily put off and respond: 'What do we have to do?'

Now His Highness thinks of a truly Emperor-like discipline, in which the people have to cover the distance: for example, hopping on one leg; floating like a bird; curtsying up and down, and so on. While they are doing this, the Emperor tries to catch as many followers as possible. The last remaining person is appointed to be the new Emperor.

(75) Sunrise

All the players are 'asleep' on the floor. Players have their eyes closed, but are allowed to peek occasionally, otherwise they would not notice the imminent sunrise. The sun appears in the form of a large, yellow cardboard circle that a chosen player holds behind his back. If he lets the yellow disk rise in the sky (by lifting it), it is a sign for all the sleepers to get up. They quickly rise from their beds, and freely walk around the room. Meanwhile, they always keep an eye on the sun, because when it goes down all the walkers have to lie down again. The person carrying the sun is thus given special powers. He can make the group move or stop as he likes – it's as clear as daylight.

Materials: cardboard 'sun'

(76) Author by Profession

Each member of the group is given several pieces of paper of the same size, as well as a selection of coloured pens. Using this equipment, they are allowed to draw a story, without being given a topic, using free associations, and independently of the picture themes of the other participants.

Children who have difficulties starting off can be given a prompt: for example, 'visit to the open-air swimming pool'; 'visit to the zoo', and so on.

The artists draw at least three scenarios from their story, each on a different piece of paper. Afterwards, the papers are stuck together with sticky tape into a mini-booklet. Finally, the painters act as authors. An adult teams up with each player, and writes down exactly what the author dictates as a text for the picture. Poor grammar or unclear expressions are not corrected. Everything should be noted down exactly as dictated by the author. Of course, group members who are able to write can do everything themselves. At the end, a short reading takes place.

Materials: paper, pens, sticky tape

77 The Hour of Truth

If a group member behaves differently from 'normal', the reason for this could be that they are unable to live in a way that would 'normally' benefit them. Do the majority of the group's activities; the demands; the 'common' interests, and so on, actually really appeal to the temperament of that group member, their talents, their needs?

The 'hour of truth' serves to allow group members to become clearer about their own interests; to find out what personal goals they have; where perhaps they may have to act a part too much, in order to conform to group norms; where too many restrictions are set, and so on.

These small and large truths can be written down without internal or external censorship. Everyone does this for themselves, and on their own. Only when problems have had a preliminary sorting out, and have been made clear in group, members' minds, does it become easier to present them to the group sensibly and without emotion.

Materials: paper, pens

78　I Present Myself

If there are members within the group who still do not know each other very well, this game will certainly get rid of remaining uncertainties. 'I present myself' is the heading of a wanted poster on the notice board.

From this wanted poster, you can get any likely or unlikely pieces of information about the respective authors. Any categories that the writer can think of are allowed to feature – from habits to plans for the future. For example:

Holly Smith
Habits: I always like sitting on the right.
Books: My favourite books are animal stories, especially about dogs.
Friends: At the moment, I have several, but I haven't got a best friend yet.
Instruments: I play the recorder, and sometimes drum on a couple of saucepans.
Culture: My favourite artist is Van Gogh.
Favourite meal: Cheese pasta with lots of onions.
Drink: I only like soft drinks; orange is my favourite.
Music: Steps are the best band.

Materials: paper, pens

(79) Bonjour Bag

Let's be honest: what is the best thing about the first day at school? Yes, a treat given to make it a special day. At least there is one ray of light on a day when one is nervous and thrown together with strange people and an unknown teacher.

But every beginning is difficult. The first experience of youth groups, clubs, homes, nurseries and so on are all looked forward to with a certain amount of anxiety. That is why, from now on, the established group gives a personal present to new arrivals: the 'bonjour bag'. This is a mini conical bag of sweets, and can be quickly made from a sheet of paper. On it is the name of the new group member and, all around it, are the signatures of all the old, regular members. And inside everyone puts a tiny, sweet surprise.

Not only does a new group member feel welcome on being given a 'bonjour bag', but the presentation also serves as an obvious sign for all group members that there will be an addition to the group. In other words, there is now someone present to whom they should give special attention in the future.

Materials: paper, pens, sweets

Artists and Their Names

Everyone can do a lot of different things. If someone claims that they can do nothing, they are either lying, or they are very unsure of themselves. 'Things I can do' is the motto of this game. Whether this involves carving toothpicks, remembering lots of jokes, or dancing the samba on stilts does not matter at all. Any skill can be named. Once all participants have had the courage to own up to their talents, they are allowed to find a suitable artist's name for themselves.

What an illustrious circle, where Bodo al Swimmer, Elizabeth Haircut, Count DI from Y, and Olga de Joke present themselves.

Order Games

Today there is often an extraordinary mess in the heads of many young people – and adults – who are not up to the increasing and multiple facets of modern life.

Every day, new and changing impressions, demands and offers; a wealth of temptations, a lack of role models, and the collapse of values hinder the structuring of our own lives considerably. Order is required – particularly an ordering of thoughts, so that they can influence our personal way of life.

This section comprises a collection of games that demand a rigorous ordering of things, as well as a categorisation of more abstract terms. Concentration, perception and memory skills are fostered as much as the sensible planning of events, thought constructs, and social processes. There are games here that are intended to help people not to get distracted from what is important amid the chaos of our lives.

81 Bailiffs Collect the Junk

If everywhere in the house (or in the garden) looks like a bomb has hit it, then it is time for the bailiffs to collect the junk. Suddenly and ruthlessly the game is announced: in a lightning operation, all group members collect anything that is lying around without a home, and put it into a basket. This basket is covered with a cloth and put on a table. The tension rises as the leader reaches into the basket with the ominous words: 'What should the owner of the junk in my hand do as a forfeit?'

The group suggests different forfeits from which the leader chooses one. Then the leader lets out the secret: the piece of junk is revealed – and with it its owner, who now has to yield to their fate and do what they are told. Whether that means that they have to say the 17 times table backwards, or do a little Russian dance, the forfeit has been paid only when the telltale item has been put away or got rid of properly. The only hope is that there won't be any more items belonging to the same person in the basket.

Materials: basket or box

82 Ki-Lou-Ba

This is a game that helps to gain a general overview of the articles, equipment or decorative items in the home, or in the group rooms. What belongs where? That is where it really should be found all the time!

In this order game, pieces of paper are used with abbreviations for all the relevant rooms written down. For example:

Ki	BR	DIY	SR
carrot	curtain	chisel	crate

Ki = kitchen
BR = big common room
DIY = DIY room
SR = store room
and so on.

Then one person recites the alphabet. A second person stops him at some point; for example, at the letter 'K'. Immediately, everyone tries to find words beginning with 'K' for the different columns. As soon as someone has found an item beginning with 'K' for each column – that is, for each room – the round has finished.

Points distribution: 20 points are given for each word; whenever two players have written the same word, they are allowed to have only five points each.

Tip: All participants should already be quite familiar with the premises, because the game relates exclusively to items that can be found there.

Materials: paper, pens

83 Housework Snap

Symbols representing clearing-up jobs are drawn on small squares of card (approximately 8 × 8 cm [3 × 3"]): laying the table; doing the dusting; sweeping; clearing snow; cleaning the bird cage, and so on.

For each card, there is an exact duplicate. Group members create as many symbol pairs as necessary. (A list of all the jobs to be done is simply divided by the number of group members.)

The finished playing cards are shuffled and, before the week begins, are spread out face-down on the table during a good-humoured group get-together. And now 'Snap' is played.

Moving around clockwise, players take it in turns to turn over a card. The cards stay uncovered. As soon as a player uncovers the twin card of a card that has already been uncovered, they shout 'Snap!', and the symbol pair belongs to them. They are now in charge of the jobs represented on the cards.

However, because it would be unfair if one player ended up taking on most of the housework, the sizes of the stacks of cards are compared afterwards. The winners are allowed to share out pairs of cards, until everyone has to do about the same weekly workload.

In any case, all participants are shown the multitude of jobs to be done, and everyone can familiarise themselves with their responsibilities within the group in a playful way.

Materials: card, scissors, pens

(84) **Throwing Waiters**

When, after a nice meal, everyone is sitting around the table with a full stomach and tired legs, and no one appears to be able to summon enough energy to clear the table, the time has come for 'throwing waiters'.

A dice is passed around. Every player throws the dice once. The number of dots on the dice corresponds to the number of items they have to clear from the culinary battlefield.

Materials: dice

85   Whistle Blowing for Jobs

When it is a question of assigning a job that is not a straightforward one – one that no one will rush to do, such as cleaning out the aquarium, repairing the tent, or painting the garden fence – then the decision is left to chance. 'Chance' leaves the room equipped with a whistle. In the room, the rest of the group organise themselves into a circle. An item typically associated with the job in question is passed in a clockwise direction from player to player. 'Chance' outside the door blows the whistle for the start. Now every participant has to quickly take the item from their neighbour, and even more quickly get rid of it to the next person because, at any time, the second whistle could sound, and the person who has got the item at that point has 'won' the job.

A little comfort: at the next job distribution, the winner is allowed to be the whistler so that, for one round at least, they are out of the woods.

Materials: whistle, various objects

86   Hansel and Gretel

Every child knows the story of the two children abandoned by their parents in a forest. The children knew about their imminent fate, because one evening when they were in bed they overheard their parents talking about their plans when they believed that the children were already asleep.

For this game, all participants imagine themselves in their beds. Everyone imagines it is evening; the door is slightly ajar, and they are listening to their parents talking. They are talking about the child (or children). What might be heard?

Everyone gets as much time as they need to write down the fictitious parental conversation. Of course, what is wanted here is not stories that are as creepy as possible, but rather a realistic evaluation of the individual parents' attitudes towards their children. Afterwards, the results can be presented and discussed.

This game is a different way of looking for order. When attitudes, expectations and views of ourselves are reflected on deliberately, it becomes easier to recognise obstacles, or to approach goals more systematically, because now many things are clearer than before.

Materials: paper, pens

87 Beer Mat Puzzles

Beer mats are collected, if possible with the same images on them. Each player has a few examples lying in front of them. Using a dark felt-tip pen, and with or without a ruler, a crooked line is drawn to divide the beer mat in two. It does not matter whether the dividing line is drawn from corner to corner, or from side to side. Using a strong pair of household scissors, players now cut along the line, and so end up with two fitting jigsaw pieces per beer mat.

Now the game can begin. All the pieces are shuffled thoroughly, and spread out across the table. The first player is allowed to try their luck. They randomly pick a piece, and then have a set time to find the matching piece. When the time is up, the pieces are shuffled anew and it is the next player's turn.

Variation: All players rummage through the mountain of jigsaw pieces together. Who has the biggest pile of loot when all pairs are complete?

Materials: lots of beer mats, felt-tip pens, scissors (rulers, possibly)

88 Logical Eggs

Using soft play dough, a really nice, big chicken's egg is formed by every player. The play dough may be mixed from different colours, which makes things more exciting! Each egg is now put in the egg cutter, and divided into slices of equal thickness. Afterwards, the flat slices are put in the freezer for approximately 10 minutes. That makes them nice and hard and good to grip, because this game is about putting one's egg together again in the shortest possible time.

The game becomes particularly difficult, but also funny, when several participants shuffle their egg slices together before they start putting their own eggs together again.

Ready, steady, go! The egg timer is set to three minutes. Anyone who has been unable to reassemble their egg has to 'lay' another egg immediately as a punishment – for the next round.

Tip: Players who are clever make some sort of subtle change to their egg along the length of it: for example, an almost invisible groove, or a small bulge.

Materials: play dough, egg cutter

89 Reaching the Destination Across Word Bridges

This game is about extracting essential pieces of text from a long account that are relevant to understanding the whole, or to filtering out information cognitively, so that later you can recall the main facts of the story in chronological order.

Every participant looks for a suitable, generally interesting and informative piece of text. They can take this from a newspaper or seek advice from an encyclopaedia. A graphic set of directions can also be reduced to a few key words. For example, this is how you get to the playing fields:

> Go along the main road until you get to the traffic lights. There you turn right. Next to the road there is a flower meadow. At the end of the meadow is a farm. At the farm, you turn left into some allotments. The path continues through a small wood. You can already see the playing fields from there.

While the description is being read out, all players note down information that they consider to be relevant. For example:

> *main road – right – farm – left – allotments –*
> *wood – playing fields*

An even shorter (and no less correct) version could be:

main – rt – cow – lt – trees – playing fields

The extent to which individuals can abbreviate facts and still remember what they mean varies a great deal. And everyone associates different mental pictures with the information given. So off we go: the shorter, the better. And whether someone has understood the 'story' will become clear when they have to reconstruct it using their notes.

Materials: newspapers, encyclopaedias, paper, pens

90 Nutolini

All the players are seated around a table. In the middle, there is a bowl of mixed nuts: peanuts, walnuts, Brazil nuts and hazel nuts, for example.

The person who starts is blindfolded and puts on a pair of thin gloves. First of all, the blindfolded player rummages about in the bowl with both hands, feeling the different shapes, and then decides on one type of nut. Will he be able to find all the nuts of that type that are in the bowl?

One point is given for every correct nut. Wrong nuts are subtracted from the total of correct nuts. The remaining points are noted down. Then it is the next person's turn.

Note: Please check that nobody is allergic to nuts before playing this game. Different pasta shapes could be used instead.

Materials: bowl, different types of nuts, paper, pen

91 The Money-Counting Board

A money-counting board is used to bring order to the group's finances. Someone who has connections with a bank may be able to get hold of a disused model. Otherwise, you can make one yourself.

First of all, all the collected coins are sorted into the same denominations and piled up in towers. Then a square base approximately 6cm (2") thick is made from soft clay, and put on to a plastic sheet. The size of the base depends on the number of coin rows needed.

Afterwards, the coins are stuck on edge one above the other, in batches of 10, into the clay base, so that half of them protrude.

The coins remain in the base until the clay has dried, so creating a practical 'toy' for budding little bankers who want to practise counting and sorting small change.

Tip: Make the slits slightly bigger than the coins because they become more narrow when the clay has dried.

Variations: Anyone who soon finds the sorting and counting too boring can develop their own funny games, by adding one or two dice. For example, whenever the sum of both dice comes up to 10, a coin to the same value can be slotted into the board.

Materials: clay, plastic foil, small change

92   Bits and Pieces Office

Nothing is more difficult to sort out than a collection of knick-knacks – lots of small or tiny articles that don't really belong anywhere. For such things, the opening of a bits and pieces office is recommended. This consists of one or several shelves, on which numerous items can be placed: empty film boxes (obtainable free of charge from photographers) for elastic bands, drawing pins, beads, paper clips, empty ink cartridges and so on; larger tins (for example, stock cube tins) for miniature animals, coloured pens, sticky tape, small change, and so on, and larger shoe boxes for secret articles of all sorts. The containers are covered with colourful paper and labelled so that one can see at a glance what is hidden inside them. Even though, in a way, the bits and pieces office may visually remind us of junk, it is nevertheless very important for children and teenagers, because they can organise their own affairs, determine the sequence, and throw out or change things around to their hearts' content – an important exercise for developing a desire to take care of one's property.

Tip: Tool boxes with drawers, as used by DIY devotees for storing screws, are very suitable too, as is a small toy shop with all its little shelves.

Materials: various containers (film boxes, other small boxes, shoe boxes, and so on), coloured paper or wrapping paper, pens, glue, scissors

93 **What is What?**

A player names any adjective – for example, 'runny', 'cold', 'fast', and so on – and participants immediately have to think of things that the adjective applies to: 'cold', for example, could apply to vanilla ice-cream, a fridge, feet and so on. Everyone is given one minute to note down all the words that they can think of. The winner is the person with the largest yield in 'cold things'.

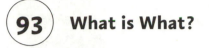

Materials: paper, pens

(94) Dumpling Post

This game is about categorisation, game speed and concentration. As preparation for the game, players agree on a number of post codes, and note them down. It would be most useful if they chose those post codes they have always wanted to remember. Each player now prepares a stack of 'letters' that they want to send. However, these are not just common letters, they are unconventional 'dumpling post', in the form of scrunched-up little paper balls. Each player chooses the paper colour they prefer.

Next, empty boxes are put out. On each box, one of the chosen post codes is written in big letters. Then the leader gives the go-ahead for the first round by calling out one of the post codes – for example, HP16 9LF.

The other dumpling postmen listen carefully; locate the correct 'post box', and aim their coloured dumpling letters into it. But they must be quick, because the next post code is already being read out, and another one, and so on. Any person who can retain an overview at that speed is very lucky.

To generally confuse matters, the leader is also allowed to call out post codes that have not actually been noted down.

Tip: If the leader makes a note beforehand of the sequence of post codes they are going to call out, it is possible, at the end of the game, to establish who reacted correctly. Because if

Amersham was called five times, Chesham three times and High Wycombe seven times, then there should be, for the player with the blue dumpling post, five blue dumplings in the Amersham box; three blue dumplings in the Chesham box, and seven blue dumplings in the High Wycombe box.

Off goes the post!

Materials: different coloured paper, empty boxes

95 Ding-Dong-Gloria

An enjoyable, and pleasant-sounding order game that involves the creation and categorisation of sounds. For this, a number of glasses containing different amounts of water are prepared, and randomly arranged on the table.

First, the test phase takes place. Each player taps each glass once with a teaspoon, and tries to remember the pitch and location of the 'instrument'. Then the real test follows. The leader has prepared two symbol cards:

⬆ = higher pitch than the preceding tone

⬇ = lower pitch than the preceding tone

The first player begins by making a sound using any of the glasses. Now the leader announces themselves by raising one of the symbol cards – for example, the upwards-pointing arrow. If the musician manages to choose a glass that indeed sounds higher than the first, he is given one sound point, and is allowed to continue until he makes a mistake. The points achieved are noted down, and a new glass tapper tries his luck.

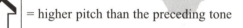

Materials: glasses, symbol cards

96 Box Lists

This is a game for outdoors. In a box, there are several different objects and bits and pieces. The whole contents are known to the leader, so they can prepare four pieces of paper, on each of which they list in writing a quarter of the objects. The lists are stuck to four trees, which are located at some distance from each other. The 'treasure chest' stands in a central place in the grass, covered with a cloth.

When the game begins, many hands reach into it at the same time (each player using one hand!) and, at a signal, take out one object. Each player quickly looks at their find – for example, a salt shaker – and tears off. On which list might their find be written down? They zoom from tree to tree, flicking over the items on the lists in the hope of having come to the correct tree. Of course, at the same time, they also superficially read the other items on the lists. People with a photographic memory are lucky here. The next round is bound to be easier for them, when players reach into the treasure chest again and then maybe have to find the list for the pipe cleaners. Where was that again? On tree one, two, three, or four?

Rules: In every round, the last person to find the list that includes their item, or who is at the wrong tree drops out. In the end, only the winner is left: the fastest runner *and* finest reader of all.

> **Materials:** various objects, box or basket, paper, drawing pins

97 Look Carefully!

This is a fiddly game for vigilant observers! On the table are a number of household items. Each participant tries to remember the exact location of the individual items. At a command, everyone except the leader closes their eyes. The leader quickly swaps over two items and then calls out: 'Open your eyes!'

Who can spot what has changed? There is applause for the player with the sharp eyes. They can be the leader for the next round.

Materials: various objects

98 The Lolly-Test

This funny categorisation game puts players' taste buds to the test. On the table, there are up to five clothes pegs, each of which grips a different flavoured sweet – a lemon sweet, one with raspberry flavour, an orange sweet, pink grapefruit, and blackcurrant, for example.

Now the game gets exciting. The first taster is blindfolded. In the meantime, the others change the order of the sweets. Now the taster can get to work. He feels for the first clothes peg, moves it to his mouth, and carefully licks the sweet up to three times. Will he be able to name the correct flavour? Excitement is likely to mount because it is not actually that easy to get the right result by only being allowed to lick the sweets.

As soon as a sweet has been guessed correctly, the player is allowed to reach for the next peg. The sweets that have already been licked, regardless of whether they have been guessed correctly or not, belong to that player. However, as soon as one flavour has not been recognised, the tester has to stop their attempt with that sweet, and it is the next gourmet's turn. Before each player's turn the number of sweets to be tasted must be made up with fresh sweets.

Materials: clothes pegs, sweets

99　Tricky Scents

This game is about discriminating and guessing different smells. The game is limited to one or two rooms. A maximum of three participants per round choose a scent: for example, vanilla flavouring from the kitchen; a few drops of lemon oil, and a perfume. Each of the scents is mixed with a little water, and put in a squirty bottle.

All other participants now leave the room, while the three chosen ones leave their scent marks at different places in the room. Afterwards, the search troops are called in. By snooping around, they have to find out where the individual scent sources are located, and guess what the smells are.

Tip: While they are spraying the scents, the scent distributors note down the number and locations of scents, so that there are no uncertainties during the solving of the tricky ones.

Materials: different scents (for example, vanilla flavouring, perfume and so on), squirty bottles

(**100**) Landscapes

This game is about visually structuring a landscape. To do this, all members spread out in the immediate environment, and use their eyes to search for a feature that can be reduced to different geometric shapes. The hedge, for example, could be seen as a long cuboid; the side view of a slide hides a triangle; the pond can be portrayed as a circle or oval, and so on. Each participant draws the found forms and lines in correct relation to each other on a sheet of paper. Then the group meets to swap pictures. Who can find out which part of the landscape someone else has put down on paper?

Materials: paper, pens

Entertaining Games

Children whine for different reasons. Maybe they are sickening for something; maybe they have been waiting too long; the weather is bad and they have to spend a lot of time in the house; their friend is on holiday; a journey appears endless, and so on. In such cases, the child is unlikely to feel particularly happy, and can become very difficult. This is a good time to pull out an entertaining game from your pocket – a game that is fun and awakens curiosity, because it appeals to a child's interest and skills.

Older children and teenagers are often plagued by awful boredom, for no obvious reason. At the beginning of puberty, they are entering a new phase of life, where mood swings and a turbulent up and down of emotions are typical. For these children it is helpful, too, to channel their surplus positive and negative energies in creatively meaningful directions, instead of using them for the dramatic consolidation of a personal crisis. Often, only a small impulse is required, and even the most serene youngsters will gratefully take up a suggestion for an exciting activity, despite the fact that, at their age, they are not actually interested in such childish stuff any more.

(101) Throwing Paper Clips

This concentration game requires a square piece of cardboard, a coloured dice, and lots of different coloured paper clips in the six colours of the dice. The paper clips are stuck next to each other all around the cardboard. Then the game can begin!

The participants form a circle, and the first player throws the dice. If the dice stops, for example, on blue, that person is allowed to take off a blue paper clip. This colour is binding for that player who, from now on, has to collect blue paper clips. Now 10 or more rounds are played, or a certain number of minutes are set on a kitchen timer. The amount of time chosen is dependent on the number of players and their ages. Each player is allowed to throw the dice twice, which increases the chance of getting the chosen colour. The paper clip winner is the person who manages to get the most paper clips in their colour by the end of the agreed time.

Materials: cardboard, coloured paper clips, coloured dice

(102) Bath Gnomes

So today is bath day? Give the little ones a roll of new toilet paper or kitchen paper instead of the obligatory rubber duck. With it, they can make something really special: generous lengths of the paper are torn off the roll, scrunched up and briefly dipped in the water. Then the lovely, slimy ball is pressed firmly against the wall tiles. Hooray! The first eye of the bath gnome sticks. Then he is given his second eye, his nose, and a wide mouth. If you want to, you can also stick on hair, so that the wall face is complete. It can stay on the wall, at least until the next day. Then the artists can admire their three-dimensional tile gnomes in a dried, hardened state. Isn't it brilliant what toilet paper can be good for!

Tip: Take a photo of the little bath monster and the tile gnome together!

Variation: In the same way, you can also let bored kids decorate fridge doors, baking trays, plastic cupboards, or even the car.

Materials: toilet paper

(103) Glossy Pictures

Children are attracted by anything that glitters and shines. So, from now on, such things must not be thrown away carelessly, but should be kept in a 'glitter box'. Things that can be collected include the golden inner containers of coffee jars; the remains of shiny Christmas foil; wrapping paper; old eye shadow or nail varnish; old reading glasses; bright drinking straws; tinsel; shiny fabric linings; glitter, and so on. The more extensive and varied the collection, the more the artists will stick with the activity. If there are also some spare photographs of group members (or the artists themselves) in stock, everything is perfect. However, just as good are glossy photographs from catalogues and advertising brochures.

Now the work begins. Depending on their interests and inclinations, the children are allowed to put together a colourful collage: for example, a human face, or an animal figure, and all around it a lot of glitter trees, stars, or simply a cut-out pattern. Very small children are often happy with just cutting strips of paper, especially if their enthusiasm is shared by the adults. Things are stuck on one after the other, preferably with a glue stick.

It does not matter at all whether the picture can be recognised as something concrete or not. It will look wonderful anyway when the artist is allowed to look at it in the dark, using a torch to shine on the sparkly work of art.

Materials: anything that glitters, round-ended scissors, glue

104 Fly-Swatter Tennis

For this game, each child needs a tennis racket – for example, a fly-swatter. Almost as suitable are a ladle, a wooden spoon, an empty paper roll, or a piece of cardboard.

The children form a circle. Then an inflated balloon is brought into the game. This balloon has to be hit from one participant to the next without being allowed to touch the floor.

If you want, you can draw a funny face on the balloon, to make the game even more fun.

Materials: fly-swatters or wooden spoons, balloon

(105) Fruit Skewers – Diced

In six bowls there are six different types of small fruit: for example, raspberries, blackcurrants, cherries, gooseberries, strawberries, and plums. Apples, bananas, pears, and so on that have been cut into small pieces are also suitable. A clear symbol is drawn for each type of fruit on to sticky labels, which are stuck to the six surfaces of a large, square brick to form a dice.

Now every participant is given a wooden skewer and then the first player throws the dice. According to the symbol that comes up, the player takes a piece of fruit from the respective bowl, and sticks it on their skewer. The game continues clockwise until every player has at least one example of each type of fruit on their skewer. Then the game is finished and the vitamin-rich loot can be nibbled off the skewers. Of course, players can also make each other skewer presents.

Materials: six bowls, six types of fruit, wooden skewers, dice, sticky labels, pens

(106) The Back Seat Pad

Something that children often cannot bear is long car journeys. This strain can be eased a little by having a back seat pad.

A piece of string to which a small tear-off note pad has been tied is attached to the headrest of the front seat. On the other support of the headrest is a piece of string with a pen attached to it. Now the mini-travellers can be better equipped for the awful journey when they are told, 'Draw all the animals that you can see during the journey'; or 'You are allowed to make a tick every time you see a *blue* car'; or 'Close your eyes and draw a "blind picture".' If someone does not feel like drawing anything, they can tear off a piece of paper, and fold it into anything they like.

Tip: If you go on a trip to the supermarket, invent symbols for the different groceries, to make sure none is forgotten.

Materials: tear-off note pad, string, pen

(107) Waving Eggs

All players require a ping-pong ball, and something wide to wave: for example, a piece of cardboard, or a plastic plate.

Pieces of string are used to mark out the beginning and end of a course that has to be crossed. Several participants start at the same time. The ping-pong balls lie on the starting line. As soon as the whistle goes, the players drive their feather-light 'eggs' along by waving their plates back and forth over them until they cross the finishing line. At no time must the plate touch the ball. Once the first 'egg' has crossed the finishing line, the winner for this round has been decided.

Tip: The game becomes more difficult if several obstacles are built into the course that players have to wave their eggs around, or through which eggs have to be rolled (for example, an empty cardboard tube).

Materials: ping-pong balls, plastic or paper plates, or wide strips of cardboard, string

108 Shooting Stars

Make a number of shooting stars from plain coloured paper by screwing it up into small balls. Each player chooses their own colour. In addition, every child needs a ruler. At an appropriate distance, a cardboard box is placed on a pedestal (for example, a foot stool). The opening of the box faces the 'shooting star throwers'. Now every participant loads their ruler with a paper ball: that is, they bend the ruler backwards, hold the missile with one hand on the upper surface of the ruler and then let go of that end of the ruler, letting fly at the cardboard box. How good individual players are at aiming can be discovered from the number of shooting stars of the same colour that are in the box.

Tip: If there is no coloured paper available, each child can mark their ammunition with a felt-tip pen dot in their own colour.

Materials: paper, several rulers, cardboard box

(109) Crocodile

The players are divided into as many 'shouting groups' as there are syllables in the word to be guessed.

First, one participant – the guesser – is sent outside. The others then decide quietly which word is to be guessed, and who is going to take on which syllable. The strange concert begins as soon as the guesser enters the room. Let us suppose the word 'crocodile' is to be guessed: the first group shouts rhythmically, 'Croc, croc, croc …', the second group 'o, o, o …' and the third 'dile, dile, dile …'. Everyone shouts at the same time and in the same rhythm, so that the poor listener does not lose their hearing altogether. Will he be able to come up with the right answer?

(110) Wool Soup

Collect balls of leftover wool, and using these and a pair of scissors, even small children can have a lot of fun, because today they are going to cook wool soup. Snip, snip: each child cuts the threads into different lengths, and stirs them well in a bowl. It will be a feast for the eyes if threads have different colours, and if there are a few glittery ones among them. The soup can be arranged on a paper plate, using liquid glue, and the dried 'dish' put on the wall.

Tip: Anyone who likes unusual additions to their soup can also search a collection of buttons for funny examples, and then stick them down as little button dumplings.

Materials: wool, bowl, round-ended scissors, liquid glue, paper plates

111 Nature Mandalas

Working together, the group prepares a master plan for an unusual mandala, put together from items from nature. A mandala ('circle') is a magic-symbolic diagram, a pictorial representation of the world, used in Hinduism and Buddhism as a meditation aid. The psychoanalyst CG Jung adopted the term as a symbol for the deep structure of the psyche which, as a circle or square, represents completeness and totality.

The arrangement of different patterns is drawn on to a big sheet of paper, and the required materials are noted down. Afterwards, the whole group goes outside to look for the agreed leaves and other materials. Of course, if someone finds something particularly unusual they can bring that back with them, too. On the pavement, the plan is then put into action. Flower heads, conkers, grass, beechnuts, leaves, stones and so on are carefully arranged into a colourful and complete nature-mandala.

Tip: Don't forget your camera!

Materials: large sheet of paper, natural materials, camera

(112) Pin the Tail

A life-size animal is drawn on to a large sheet of paper. Any animal that has a tail can be chosen, but the tail is omitted from the drawing, because players must put it on themselves, using string or a piece of wool and sticky tape. What could be easier? Except the players are blindfolded before they go into action! Now they have to rely totally on their instincts and their ability to remember: approximately where would the bottom of an elephant be? By guesswork, each player sticks the tail on the animal.

Rules:
◆ Anyone who misses the animal altogether gets no points.
◆ If the animal is hit somewhere on its body, one point is given.
◆ Three points are given when the right side of the body has been hit.
◆ The winner, with five points, is the person who was best able to place the tail.

Tip: Put names on the tails prior to the start of the game.

Materials: large sheets of paper, pens, strings or pieces of wool

(113) Small Miracles

Each participant requires a jar top that has been filled with a ball of play dough. For their 'small miracle', everyone then sets off to find a particularly decorative small twig. The twig is pushed into the play dough, and then participants move on to the creative individual dressing of the dwarf tree.

No limits are set to the imagination. Maybe someone wants to stick confetti all over their twig? 'Fruits' of any kind are possible, as long as they are tiny enough: little paper balls; apples made from red play dough; pieces of thread; 'real' children's jewellery such as rings; nature treasures such as beechnuts; small rose hips; daisy heads or, of course, cotton wool snow for the winter.

These are fixed to the 'trees' using glue, or are simply tied on. Now the group can have Christmas trees all year round.

Materials: jar tops, play dough, small twigs, various tree decorations

114 Raisin Man

To make raisin men, you will need toothpicks and, of course, a lot of raisins. Larger varieties or prunes are especially good. They can be shaped by hand until they change their flat form and look more three-dimensional. Now they can be used as heads, 'double tummies', threesome arms and legs, by skewering them on to the toothpicks. Finally, the little men are given funny faces using tiny drops of food colouring, or stuck-on hundreds and thousands.

Each little man is given two little shoes made from play dough. In this way, the whole raisin family can survive for several generations.

Materials: lots of raisins, toothpicks, food colourings or hundreds and thousands, play dough

(115) Soap Operas

Two equally strong groups put their skills and reactions to the test. Two teams form a circle. In the middle rules the 'soap master', who has a new piece of soap and a bucket of water. Ready, steady, go! The soap master briefly dips the soap into the water and then squeezes it with both hands so as to send it to one of the players in the circle. If that player is able to catch the slimy flying object, the group is given one point. A further point is given if the successful catcher can send the soap back to the 'master' who also manages to catch it. The piece of soap moves round in a clockwise direction, between the soap master and the next player, back and forth, until it has done the round once. If the soap falls on the floor, a point is lost.

Instead of having a win on points, you can also play against the clock. The faster group wins. If the soap falls on the ground, the throw has to be repeated as many times as are needed for that player to catch the soap, then the round is continued.

By the way, 'soap operas' work best outside, when it is sunny and the players are in swimming costumes.

Materials: pen, piece of soap, bucket

(116) Knot Race

Between 10 and 20 marks are made at regular intervals on two tracks on the grass using, for example, coloured cones, twigs or fir cones. Two teams line up for the competition. The first runner of each team carries a knotted scarf in their hand. At the sound of the whistle they run off. As soon as they get to the first mark, they put down the knot and then run on to the last mark. They then turn around and run back to their team, where they give the second runner a starting signal by slapping their hand. The second runner sets off immediately, snatches up the knot at the first mark, runs on and drops the knot at the second mark. They then continue their run as described above, and then send off the third runner, who carries the knot to the third mark; the fourth person will take it to the fourth mark, and so on.

If players are tired, the game finishes once the last mark has been reached. Fit players, however, also carry the knot back in the same way: runner by runner, mark by mark, back to the start. The winner is the first group to complete.

Materials: way markers (for example, cones or twigs), scarves

117 The Water Bomb Track

A long track of plastic sheeting is laid down outside. Old tarpaulins are perfectly suitable for this. Holes can simply be mended with sticky tape. In addition, each participant needs a water-filled balloon – a different colour for each player. Then the tarpaulin is sprayed with water so that the colourful bombs will slide better.

Participants approach the start in bowling fashion, one at a time; they set off, bend down and then throw. See who can manage to place their water bomb as close as possible to a stone placed on the track.

Tip: Sprinkling a little wallpaper glue on to the track increases the sliding speed tremendously!

Variations:
◆ Two players compete at the same time. Whose missile will slide faster?
◆ Two players stand facing each other at opposite ends of the track. Can they manage to get their bombs to crash into each other?

Materials: plastic sheets (tarpaulins, plastic bags), sticky tape, different-coloured balloons filled with water

(118) Welcome to Robert's Crafty Club

To become a member of the crafty club, you have to fulfil certain conditions. The task is to be crafty enough to find out what Robert likes and what he does not like at all. Someone in the know gives some examples:

◆ Robert likes horse riding, but he does not like swimming
◆ Robert loves radishes, but not chips
◆ Robert loves running, but does not like being sweaty.

Now it is the other players' turn to name things that might meet Robert's taste. Anyone who sees through the system is allowed to join the crafty club without telling others the answer and think of new joining conditions for future rounds. The answer: Robert only likes things beginning with R; anything else he is not at all interested in.

Further ideas:
Debbie's club only likes things that have double letters in their name.
Sonja's club prefers things ending in 'a'.

(119) Relay Pen

Two teams compete against each other at the same time. Players stand one behind the other, the first player holding a pen. Some distance away, there are two posters on the floor, one for each team. The aim is to run there as quickly as possible and write down a word. But not just any word. Just before the start, the leader announces the heading for this round. For example, if the leader calls out 'vegetables', the first team member runs over to the paper with the pen, thinking of a vegetable, and then writes the name down on the poster: for example, 'cabbage'. Quickly they run back and pass the pen to the next person who, in turn, runs off and adds another vegetable, 'carrots', for example. In the end, the different types of vegetables written down by each team are compared. Each correct word is worth one point, but where the same vegetables have been written down twice, *both* have to be taken off the final total.

Other headings could include toys, makes of car, book titles, clothes, plants, mushrooms, or fruit.

Materials: two posters (large pieces of paper), pens

(120) Cuckoo in the Nest

All players except one are seated in a semi-circle next to each other. Opposite them, the 'cuckoo' sits on the floor. The cuckoo has prepared several folded-up pieces of paper bearing a number – one piece of paper for each player. Because each number features twice, two participants at a time will get the same number. Players take it in turns to draw a number from a hat or bag. However, the numbers drawn are kept secret. In particular, the cuckoo must not know who has received which number. The cuckoo now has to find out who has which number by calling out one number: for example, '2'. Because, initially, one '2' will not know the identity of the other '2', they have to communicate as inconspicuously as possible, using body language. Then they very quickly swap seats. The cuckoo, however, has to try to pre-empt them, and sit down in someone else's nest. If the cuckoo manages to get to one of the two chairs before a '2' was able to sit down, they are allowed to stay there, and the stranded player is appointed as the new cuckoo.

After a few rounds, the number partners who belong together should generally be known, so that getting to the nest first is only a matter of concentration and speed.

Variation: To make the game more difficult, the cuckoo can call out two different numbers.

Materials: paper, pens, hat or bag

Learning Games

School is often a drag. Having to get up early; doing long hours of concentrated work; having to put up with boring teachers; tricky exam questions, and time-consuming homework – school has much to offer to make pupils' lives a misery, to say nothing of hated subjects where learning is most difficult. And yet children also learn their attitude towards school. A determining factor is how role models, such as parents, siblings, aunts and friends, talk about school, and how much they like or liked going there themselves. Statements such as 'I am more worried about my daughter's first day at school than she is', 'The other teacher would have been much better for my Tony', or 'I was never very good at history, and Sally now is exactly the same' tend to cause fear, reluctance or timid behaviour in children, instead of actually preparing them for the seriousness of life.

It is much better to share in a child's experiences at school, and not just in the role of homework guardian or strict resident teacher who cheerlessly swots up vocabulary! The best role model for pupils is a curious, enthusiastic person who recognises the positive aspects of learning. If this person also comes down from their exalted position of cleverness, maturity and experience, in order to sit on the school bench themselves – at least in a game – this can only serve to motivate. Why shouldn't group games also be learning games, as long as fun and excitement are guaranteed? School is fun: that is the motto of this section. There is something in it for everyone. With a little bit of variation, the following games can also be used for different age groups.

(121) News Bingo

This game will soon show who is politically up-to-date! All the players sit down in front of the television to watch the daily news together. One of them – the scribe – is equipped with paper and pen, and takes notes on all the important information in the form of key points. The others are not allowed to look at the notes, because they are supposed to remember the news as well as they can without any written memory aids. After the programme, the scribe takes the first player next door into the 'bingo room'. There, the scribe and player sit opposite each other. The player now begins to list systematically all the news that he can remember. As soon as a statement corresponds to one of the scribe's points in terms of content, the scribe nods approvingly and puts the player's initials next to the corresponding piece of information. Should the same player actually recall all the information on the scribe's list, the scribe shouts out 'Bingo'.

The next player is called in. Can he match the performance of his predecessor? If there are several winners at the end of the game, all of whom got the complete set of answers, a knockout competition is held. Who is quickest to answer a question about a news programme a couple of days ago?

Materials: television, paper, pens

(**122**) Toes Dictation

Of course, children have to practise a lot until newly learned words from spelling tests have really sunk in. You may be able to tempt real spelling grouches with the following funny practice variation. Each participant sits on the floor with bare feet. With a felt-tip pen between their toes, they now have to write in capital letters on a large sheet of paper. The leader dictates the words to be learned for that week.

Materials: large sheet of paper, felt-tip pens

(123) Pulling Something out of Thin Air

Each group member writes down any word they like on a piece of paper. All the pieces of paper are put into a bag and shuffled well.

The first two players reach into the bag. Each of them draws out two pieces of paper, so that they have between them, for example: car, peach, Italy, plague. The pair read out the words they have drawn, and then have five minutes to invent a story using those words. The remaining participants, too, use the time to get busy writing their own stories.

When the time is up, the starter pair present their story. The following reading of all the other stories containing the same words should not be used to make comparisons. However, we may be amazed at the multitude of different ideas.

Materials: paper, pens

(124) Balloon Mathematics

Balloon mathematics is a maths game where, first of all, pairs have to be formed. One player from each pair is to get stuck into the balloon fight, while the second player takes up an observational position and records on a notepad the balloon hits their partner scores.

The active players gather in no particular order in the middle of the room. Now a lot of inflated and labelled balloons are brought into the game. Each balloon has a number written on it in dark felt-tip pen. (The choice of numbers depends on the age and counting ability of the respective group.) Then balloons start to fly across the room in all directions. Everyone who is confronted with a balloon hits out and knocks the balloon as far away from them as possible – but, at the same time, the balloon number has to be registered and memorised because, as soon as the next balloon comes flying along, its number has to be added to the preceding one; and so on.

The observer in the background must not miss anything either. They note down the number of each balloon that their partner has touched. At the end of the playing time, a comparison is made: does the sum the fighter has worked out in their head correspond to the sum of all the numbers noted down on the piece of paper by their observer?

Materials: paper, pens, balloons, felt-tip pens

(125) Clothes Pegs Tables

In a basket there are a lot of labelled wooden clothes pegs. On each clothes peg there is a number between one and 20. In addition, each playing couple requires a strip of cardboard with a grid drawn on it.

On hearing the starting signal, both players reach into the basket and take out a clothes peg. The two clothes pegs are clipped opposite each other on to the first box of the grid: for example, peg 5 and peg 12. Now players have to multiply quickly. Who will be first to give the right answer? The fastest person in this round is allowed to leave his peg where it is; the other player removes his peg and puts it back in the basket. The winner is the player who at the end of the game has more pegs on his side of the cardboard strip.

Materials: wooden clothes pegs, basket or similar, cardboard strips

(126) Language Pairs

Each group member produces a number of memory pairs. For this, a lot of identical strips of card are cut and labelled with different words. Using a dictionary, everyone now finds the German or French equivalent word and writes them on a twin piece of card. This way, an extensive and unlimited collection of matching memory pairs is created that will make a brilliant group game. Who can get the most pairs?

With this game, learning is even attractive to those foreign-language grousers.

Tip: For younger children, the English term can be accompanied by a picture. Even though they may not yet be able to read the foreign word, foundations will be laid for a feeling for the sound of the new language.

Materials: cardboard, dictionary, pens

(127) Reporter 'P'

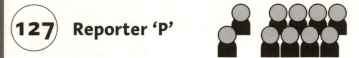

Each player has a page from an old newspaper in front of them. One player is appointed reporter and, mentally, runs through the alphabet. A second player stops him, for example, at the letter 'P'. Quickly, everyone begins searching. Using a pen, squiggles are put around as many P's as can be found on that page of text. Who can show the most squiggles?

Tip: More practised readers already differentiate between upper- and lower-case letters.

Materials: an old newspaper, pens

(128) Approximately Roughly

All players are seated in a circle around a large sheet of paper. Everyone draws a line of random length, then the pens are put down. One after the other, participants now have to give a length estimation for each line in centimetres or millimetres. Then a ruler is used to measure exactly. Who was closest in their estimate to the actual length of their line? Ten points await the 'estimation master' in each round.

Materials: large sheet of paper, pens, rulers

(129) Flea Market

Writing adverts can be good fun, when you proceed as follows:

Each player is given a piece of paper on which they note point 1 of their sale advertisement, their wanted advertisement or their swap deal. For example:

1   *The item*

As the next player is not supposed to know what object the advertisement is about, the piece of paper is folded over, a 2 is written down on the next line and then the piece of paper is passed to the next player, who writes:

2   *What the item is used for*

He folds back the piece of paper, numbers the next line with 3, and passes it on. The two remaining points of the advertisement are written in the same way:

3   *Something special about the item*

4   *Its price (or what it could be swapped for).*

At the end of the game, the flea market advertisement is unfolded and read. For example:

Suzy Bankrupt: I swap

1 False eye lashes

2 for the preparation of goat's cheese

3 covered in many flowers

4 for a colourful air bed

(130)   Numbers Clap

In the following game, participants have to call their thoughts to order:

There is a leader, the 'clapper', who, by clapping, conveys a number to the other players. The listeners count the number of claps and note down the total on a piece of paper. For example: 8. After that there follows a second and then a third clapping solo with, say, four and nine claps. Now the three-figure number is complete: 849.

The game is started slowly, then the pace of clapping is speeded up to fast and very fast. Finally, see who can remember the three-figure number without having to write it down.

Materials: paper, pens

(131) Squeaky Clean

A detective task for owners of magnifying glasses!

Using a very fine pencil, everyone writes down lots of funny, boring, or factually informative sentences, one under the other, on a piece of paper. Anything will do, as long as it meets the following three conditions:

1 Each sentence has to include at least one grammatical or spelling mistake.

2 The sentences should be neatly written and should be legible.

3 The writing must be so minute that one actually needs a magnifying glass to read what is written.

Then the pages covered in mini-sentences are photocopied – as many copies as there are players. The group leader decides whose work is going to be investigated first. The relevant photocopies are distributed among the participants. Each player now has the same piece of work in front of him, a blank sheet of paper to cover it up and, of course, a magnifying glass. As soon as the document is received, it is covered totally with the blank sheet of paper, so that particularly motivated detectives cannot begin their investigation too early. Then the author of the text gives the starting signal. Sentence 1 is to be read and searched for errors, using the magnifying glass.

Anyone who thinks they have spotted all the mistakes quickly speaks up. If they are right, they are given a 'magnifying glass point' for the correct answer. However, if they have made an error or overlooked something, they are allowed only to think during the analysis of the second sentence, but not to speak up. From sentence 3 onwards, everything is back to normal, and they can once again join in the competition to be the fastest marker.

Materials: paper, pencils, magnifying glasses

(132) Knee-Bends Tables

Off we go for some fun multiplication! All players stand in a semi-circle, with their arms stretched out in front of them. The starter says any number between one and 20: for example, five, then performs a perfect knee-bend, but only one. The next player now works out the result of two times five, calls out the answer and subsequently does two knee-bends; their neighbour knows exactly what three times five comes to. They call out the result and do three knee-bends. And so on: the five-times table is continued in this way until 10 times five.

But beware! Anyone who does not pay attention and makes a mistake working out the answer must, in order to get the blood circulation going to their brain, do as many knee-bends as would have accompanied the correct answer, following the motto: what you haven't got in your head, you have to have in your legs!

(133) Short Stories

This game is about formulating statements related to a particular word in the form of a few sentences, and writing them down in an appealing way.

The principle is very simple. Every player thinks of a word and writes it on a piece of paper. The words can be concrete or abstract terms. The pieces of paper are folded up and put into a little basket. Now everyone draws out a piece of paper and disappears into a quiet corner. All participants can take as much time as they need to compose a comprehensible piece of text of a good standard. Afterwards, the group gets together and results are presented individually and appreciated, criticised or enriched in the following discussion.

Tip: Younger players can say rather than write what they can think of with regard to a particular word.

Materials: paper, pens, little basket or something similar for the folded-up pieces of paper

134 The Kinder® -Egg Stock Exchange

At the Kinder®-egg stock exchange, all the collected plastic containers from Kinder®-eggs are distributed with new contents: in one little container there is a German sentence that has to be translated into English; in the next there might be a question about last week's history lesson; yet other eggs contain tricky maths questions; and so on. Type and level of questions depend on ability and the subjects studied at school by the participants.

The newly prepared eggs are offered in a bowl, for example, for pudding after a group meal. Everyone – including the adults, of course – reaches into the bowl once to take their 'pudding', and solves the task contained within. This way, the popular surprise eggs are turned into intellectually nourishing practice eggs.

Materials: surprise egg containers or film canisters, paper, pens

(135) Secret Words

All participants have a longish strip of paper in front of them, which they label with a word in printed letters. Then everyone folds over their strip so that only the last two letters can be seen, and passes it on to their neighbour, who tries to think what that word may have been, and adds another word that could work as a word-composite. For example:

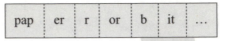

| pap | er | r | or | b | it | … |

As soon as the strip is full up with writing it is unfolded. A funny chain of composite words has been created. Whether the composites make any sense is decided by the team of players during joint reading of the results.

Materials: paper, pens

136 My Special Subject

When children talk about their 'special subject', they assume the role of a reporter who knows exactly what they are talking about. It does not matter which topic is chosen. Children can talk about looking after a dog, star constellations in the sky, comics, building a stone castle, special spelling rules, or any other elements of a typical school curriculum. The main thing is that they have fun and they are being heard. Different media can be chosen to support the presentations. In every case, they should use a notice board and a pointer. The former serves to present the topic visually to the audience and the latter can be used to point out supplementary tasks, accompanying pictures or illustrations. When, finally, the reporter is identified by a name label (sticky label) as an expert in their field, the special presentation becomes a visually important affair, too.

Materials: notice board, pointer, sticky labels, various materials

(137) The Book of Knowledge

As a rule, during conversations about school, we go on about instances where someone has not done well: a failed school test, for example; sloppy homework; not enough practice … always the same old song. Will this ever change, educationalists ask themselves (often with good reason).

Maybe we need to approach the task differently! Today, the big 'book of knowledge' is going to be opened. It consists of a book or booklet with a decorated cover. On the cover, the title is written in big letters, and inside the new things each group member has learned are noted daily. What was learned at school or outside of school today that was not known yesterday? This can be exciting. For every new item, a coloured dot is also stuck into the booklet.

No one is going to shout, 'I'll do it!' when a volunteer is called for to give a lecture, but when new knowledge is visibly appreciated, taken note of, and even highlighted by giving points, everyone is likely to dive in.

Materials: empty book or booklet, paper, coloured sticker dots

138 The All-Round Rally

The 'all-round rally' requires a little preparation. Bearing in mind the level of ability of the participants, the leader comes up with any number of general questions on different subjects or areas of interest. Particularly motivating are those questions that involve some sort of search or research task. For example:

◆ How far is it from the garage drive to the apple tree? Measure it.
◆ What is the German word for 'vacuum cleaner'?
◆ In the garden there is a plant with purple flowers and heart-shaped leaves. Look for it, bring back a leaf and, in an appropriate book, find out its name and some other details about it.
◆ In which country would you find a city called Barcelona?
◆ What shoe size does your PE teacher take?
◆ Work out the maths problem on page 15 in your maths textbook.

Adding riddles or humorous questions increases the enjoyment of the game considerably. It will be interesting to see what answers participants will have come up with when everyone meets at an agreed time and place at the end of the rally.

Materials: paper, pen

(139) Letters Quiz

This spelling game requires letter dice. You can either use already labelled dice from an existing game or a felt-tip pen to write the letters of the alphabet on to sugar cubes.

Get ready to start! Depending on the level of ability, one, two, three or more dice are used. Quickly, a word needs to be found containing all the letters thrown, but everyone should wait until the slowest player, too, has come up with a result. The maximum number of points depends on the number of players. For example, if there are six players, the fastest 'word finder' is given six points. The second-fastest gets five points, and so on. The number of points achieved is recorded individually by each player themselves. Of course, after each round, the spelling of all word creations has to be checked for correctness. Only then do the points count.

Materials: letter dice, paper, pens

(140) Book Scales

Together, the group competes in a reading competition of a special kind. First of all, all participants are put on bathroom scales and weighed. The weight of the heaviest participant represents the starting point for the competition. Let us suppose the heaviest person weighs 69 kg. The question is: how much time will the group need to digest a book mountain also weighing 69 kg?

Each book that has been read by a group member is put on the scales and its weight is noted on a record sheet. Of course, it would be particularly impressive if all the books could remain on the scales and pile up until the goal has been achieved. As a reward for the whole group, something like a visit to the cinema could be offered, for example, to see the film version of an interesting children's or teenagers' book.

Tip: Obviously, the books could simply be put down without having been read. To prevent this kind of cheating, each player has to write a brief summary after reading a book, and keep the piece of paper (dated) somewhere safe. In this way, it is possible afterwards to find out what sort of contributions individual group members have made.

Materials: bathroom scales, lots of books, paper, pens

Leisure Games

Finally, it is Friday! The last working or school day of the week has arrived; a long, free weekend is in sight. At last there is time for joint activities and outings.

However, it is often at weekends in particular that unexpected rows blow up within a group or family. Particularly on public holidays, many people lack the workday structure that they are used to; everyone gets 'on top of each other', and no one quite knows what to do with themselves. All it needs is for the weather to turn nasty, the planned outing to the open-air swimming pool to be cancelled, and everyone's mood hits rock bottom. Frequently, such a day will end in lively emotional outbursts, with everyone giving each other a piece of their minds.

What can we do? Easy: you say what is on your mind (see 'Awareness Games'); you make up (see 'Reconciliation and Rest Games'), and then look up the last section of this book! This contains many colourful games for joint leisure time – regardless of whether it is raining, the sun is shining, or it is snowing!

Happy weekend!

141 Cherry Diving

In the middle of the table there is a bowl filled with water. Lots of red, ripe cherries are floating in the water. Yummy! Don't worry – this game is not about bottling fruit. It is about diving for fruit. To do this, all participants stand in a circle around the bowl. The first player puts his arms behind his back and bends forward. Then he dips into the water with his mouth open and tries to catch a cherry with his lips or teeth. He is then allowed to enjoy eating the cherry, but he must keep the stone in his mouth. Then it is the next player's turn. Once all the players have been successful, the water is emptied out. Each cherry stone owner steps back a metre and now the spitting starts. Who can get their stone into the bowl?

This is a game that is particularly suitable for hot summer days. Of course, if there are enough participants, two groups can compete with each other – timed, of course.

Good luck!

Caution: Remind players to be careful not to swallow any cherry stones. This game is not suitable for young children as they are in danger of swallowing and choking on the cherry stones.

Materials: bowl, cherries, water

Concrete Cake with a Kick

A concrete cake is a group's most indestructible piece of art. The first thing needed for this is a 'cake board' – any wooden board will do. Four strips of wood approximately 10cm (4") high are nailed onto this board to form a frame. This monumental 'cake' is then filled with concrete. This can also be made with plaster of Paris.

Ingredients for the cake mix
◆ Fine sand or aggregate (you are aiming for a smooth finish – ask at a building site!)
◆ Cement
◆ Water
◆ Plaster of Paris

Preparation
On a cardboard base, four parts sand/aggregate and one part cement are mixed dry. Using a small shovel, the mix is then formed into a heap, in the top of which a hollow is made. Then water is slowly poured into the hollow, allowed to soak in, and then mixed again until a doughy sort of mass has been created. Alternatively, mix the plaster of Paris as instructed.

Afterwards, the concrete dough is poured into the wooden frame and shaken until smooth. As soon as the concrete is beginning to set, each group member steps into the dough once with their feet, in precise order or randomly.

well. He should be home tonight or tomorrow." He makes a face, and I know what he's going to say.

"When do I have to go?" The blood drains from my face when I think about having to see those people again.

Mark downs his beer. "Cole is trying to get you out of it. We're hoping you can do it from here using video chat, but it would be more effective if you were there in person."

"I'll do it," I say, tossing the towel aside. "Tell Frank I'll come to Washington."

"You don't have to, Sav—"

"I should get back to my customers. It was really nice seeing you, Mark. Please say hello to everyone for me." I start to walk away, but Mark hooks my arm and stops me.

"Come by the house tomorrow night and have dinner with us."

I shake my head. "Sorry, I'm working."

"Then during the day?"

"I'll see," I pat his arm and leave to tend to the rest of the customers.

"You did great tonight," Jake says a few hours later as he tugs the strap of his bag over his head. "Can I walk you out?"

"Sure." We step out into the freezing air, and tiny snowflakes wander down from the sky. I wrap my scarf around my neck. "How long have you been working for Zack?"

Jake starts walking in my direction. "For about three years. I don't have any family here, so he's taken me under his wing. I see he's done the same with you." I nod, feeling very at ease with Jake.

Underneath, they scratch their initials with a small stick. This produces a splendid piece of art, once the cake has hardened and is taken out of the wooden frame. The footprints can be decorated with paint and varnish.

Caution: Make sure everyone washes their feet before the concrete sets on them!

Tip: Using this process, fantastic group works can be created that can even fulfil a function: for example, a bird bath, seats or even hand-made bricks.

Materials: wooden board, lengths of wood, fine sand/ aggregate, cement, water, paints, varnish

(143) Catching Fleas

Fifty (or more) little fleas are drawn on to a page of a drawing pad. All the players are seated around the table, each holding a different-coloured pen in their hands. The first person to have a go is blindfolded. The leader gives the command: ready, steady, go! The 'blind' person immediately begins their hunt by quickly and arbitrarily making 10 little circles on the piece of paper. There should be exactly 10 circles – no more, no less. Afterwards, the blindfold is taken off and the player's booty is counted. One point is given for each flea that has been caught inside a circle.

Rule: Only intact fleas are awarded points! Fleas that have been cut in half, or even just touched by a circle, do not count.

Materials: drawing pad, pens, blindfold (for example, a scarf)

144 Therapy Cards

Blank cards are cut and distributed among the participants before the game begins. Ask the group therapeutic-type questions, such as, 'What is a good way of letting off steam?' Correct: being allowed to 'roar like a lion'! This can be the suggestion on the first therapy card; the person who came up with the idea writes it on one of their cards.

Each person collects up to 10 such funny therapeutic ideas, and then the game starts. The well shuffled cards lie face-down in a stack in the middle of the table. The first player takes a card and reads the 'therapeutic' suggestion. Then they act out the suggestion. The others try to guess what the card said. Moving clockwise, players take it in turns to take a playing card. However, no one is obliged to take a card in each round, and no one has to carry out the written suggestion. They can simply put the card back in the middle of the pack. After several rounds, you might want to approach the affair a little more seriously by extending the collection with further cards containing more sensitive questions, or suggestions that have some depth.

Materials: small cards, pens

145 Midnight Tree Party

On a mild summer evening, everyone is awaiting the first sign of darkness, because today there is going to be a tree party. For this, everyone collects a torch and equips themselves with a warm blanket or a cushion to sit on. Further items are required that can be used to make quiet noises: for example, a key ring; wide blades of grass for grass whistles; crisps or something similar that make a crunching sound when bitten; a mouth organ, and so on.

Now it becomes romantic: all the torches are switched on and propped up against trees or bushes so that their beams shine up into the tree tops. A few people gather around each light and make themselves comfortable on their cushions. As soon as everyone has become quiet, sounds can be heard coming from different groups. Which corner is the whistling sound or the meowing coming from; who is making a sound with their keys?

Perhaps the evening could conclude with guitars and folk songs.

Materials: torches, blankets, cushions, materials for making sounds

146 Dandelion Family

This game is used to create a symbol for the group's togetherness. Each member of the 'group family' is given a little pot filled with earth. Then the group goes and looks for dandelion seeds outside. From the seed balls, everyone picks one little seed and plants it in their pot. Each gardener labels their pot with their name in large letters. Finally, the pots belonging to Sally, John, Paul and the rest, as well as the group leader, are watered well and put on the window sill. Every participant is officially required to take on responsibility for the growing of the plant group, until the complete dandelion family is flowering in sunny yellow.

Tip: Rover, the dog, should also get a little plant, otherwise he may be offended. Other seeds can also be used, eg, sunflowers.

Materials: little plant pots, felt-tip pens

(147) Group T-shirts

For this game, each group member sacrifices a plain-coloured T-shirt. In addition, a good colour selection of felt-tip fabric pens is required with which the T-shirts can be decorated. To ensure that the colour is not going to leak through to the back, something impermeable (for example, a plastic bag) can be put inside the item of clothing to be worked on. Then each person writes their name on their T-shirt in big letters. The names can be decorated or framed. The shirt is then passed on to the next person, who immortalises their signature on the fabric. In addition, they think of a little picture or a symbol to draw that has something to do with their friendship with the shirt owner. A third group member adds their signature, and so on. A shirt like this is made for each member, and can be worn with pride on special occasions or every day.

Materials: plain T-shirts, felt-tip fabric pens, impermeable material (for example, plastic bags)

(148) Grass Indians

The grass Indians are a people who are very close to nature, and who have a particular tradition at the time of grass flowering. Each tribal member puts lots of little pigtails in their hair. Boys and girls put hair elastics around individual strands of hair. Whether these are plaited or not is left to the taste of the individual. Wearing their pigtails, the group goes off outside, where they help each other to decorate their pigtails by adding grasses, little flowers and twigs. Any natural jewellery should have a little stalk that can be stuck into the elastics. Stronger stalks will last longer than more bendy ones. As soon as participants have transformed themselves into impressive grass-flower Indians, a euphoric wood and meadow dance takes place.

Tip: Don't forget your camera!

Materials: hair elastics, camera

149 Throwing Little Stars

Each participant chooses one of the numbers on a dice as their lucky number. They note down this number as a 'heading' on a piece of paper. Now a kitchen timer is set to a particular time: the more players there are, the more minutes. Then the game starts. One after the other, players quickly throw the dice. As soon as someone hits on their lucky number, they are allowed to draw themselves a little star on their piece of paper.

The winner is the person who can show the most stars at the sound of the timer.

Materials: dice, kitchen timer, paper, pens

150 Smile, Please!

Nowadays, most households own a video camera, or at least people are likely to know someone who owns one. As soon as it is loaded, it is time for 'Action!' Each group member is allowed to show off a particular act, even if this only entails them wiggling their ears. For one day, everything is recorded that the group would like to remember later on; for example, everyone at the table; the group leader anointing his bald head with sun lotion; acrobatic feats; pulling faces; the walk to the duck pond, and so on. Particularly motivated young film-makers can make visually appealing posters with titles for the respective scenarios. These texts can be held in front of the camera, and give the group film a professional air.

So – smile, please!

Tip: Video cameras can also be rented by the day at some hi-fi and video shops.

Materials: video camera, blank tape

(**151**) Bubblegum Billiards

A table top (or a large board) is equipped with approximately 6cm (2") high cardboard strip borders (see diagram); little bits of sticky tape are sufficient to fix the card on both sides. Then the borders are broken up by simply cutting gaps into them – as many gaps as there are players. Beneath each gap, a plastic cup is attached to the lower part of the table, also using sticky tape.

This is the billiard table. Now, all you need is a good number of bubblegum balls or glass marbles, and a few cues in the form of sticks. Then players are allowed to take aim: each player decides on a particular gap – the 'pocket', into which they try to sink the ball. The best player the person with the highest number of balls in their chosen cup.

Tip: Label individual cups with players' names, to avoid later uncertainties.

Materials: smooth table top or large board, strips of cardboard, sticky tape, scissors, sticks, plastic cups (for example, yogurt pots), bubblegum balls or marbles

(152) Copy My Gesture

All participants form a circle. One person starts by making a clear gesture, or miming an expression. Their neighbour then has to copy the gesture, and also think of a second one to add to it. The third player takes on the preceding double gesture, and adds yet another one, which is taken on by the fourth participant who, in turn, invents a new one, and so on: grin-jump, jump-sob, sob-wink, wink-nod …

Now all you need to do is to imagine an unknowing passer-by looking in through the window and witnessing this strange ceremony!

Tip: Practised face-pullers can also introduce the following rule: players must first repeat all the preceding grimaces and gestures before they can introduce add their own!

(153) Balloon Relay

In the middle of the lawn a blanket is spread out. Each participant requires an inflated balloon and a small balloon filled with water. Both are labelled with the name of the respective player (use a felt-tip or ball-point pen).

Now all inflated balloons are placed at an approximately equal distance from the blanket. By throwing their water bomb, each player tries to propel their own balloon forward. Of course, this makes the lighter balloons move quickly. However, with skill and patience it is possible to advance the balloon bit by bit towards its goal. The winner is the first person to land their balloon on the blanket.

Materials: blanket, balloons, felt-tip or ball-point pen, water

---

154 The Restaurant of Enjoyment

Anyone who fancies a good get-together, and who has a good appetite is welcome at the 'restaurant of enjoyment'.

The restaurant is opened on a demand basis. Two or three group members at a time take on the organisation. After all, favourite meals must be discovered, recipes chosen, groceries bought, the chef and helpers chosen, and so on. Then the work starts. However, it is not just the meals that matter. This restaurant pays a lot of attention to the ambience: how about coloured lanterns, home-decorated napkins, plate decorations made from chocolates with little jam and whipped cream hats, or edible name cards made from rice paper written on with food colouring? There are no limits to the imagination because, in the 'restaurant of enjoyment' all boring conventions can be broken, and new means of enjoyment be found. A really bright idea could be pieces of apple decorated with sparklers served for pudding.

Bon appétit!

Materials: groceries desired, various decorations

(155) Lucky Window

A lucky window is a normal window that has been decorated to brighten up a dull and rainy day.

Finger paints can be used to create fantastic cloud effects, or snow landscapes and, in-between, brightly coloured mosaics can be made from colourful, cut-up plastic bags (sticking them to transparent bases prevents having to scrape off the remains of glue later). Using thin pieces of string, mobiles made from metal foil can be dangled from the window frame. Drawings work particularly well when they are made on clear foil using special marker pens, and are then integrated into the colourful background. The window sill could be decorated with painted and varnished stones, and dry flower arrangements mounted in play dough. Glitter affixed with wallpaper glue never fails to have an effect on a window pane.

When complete, the whole group can make itself comfortable in front of the window, and it can rain outside as much as it wants. Not many people are lucky enough to enjoy such a view!

Tip: Using a special glass scraper, most artificial remains can be removed without any problems, and the window pane will be ready and waiting for another day.

> **Materials:** finger paints, plastic bags, string, metal foil, marker pens, and so on

(156) Plaiting

An exciting and funny way to pass time is the making of ribbon plaits. Sounds too boring? Well, the attraction of the activity lies in its new technique. In this game, the left hand of one person plaits in tandem with the right hand of another. The players' idle hands have to be hidden behind their backs. Which pair is going to be able to plait the most even and the longest plait without cheating?

Tip: The ribbons are held together by a knot and tied to the back of a chair or something similar to provide a fixed starting point.

Materials: ribbons in different colours

(157) Street Painter

In order to do some street painting, each group requires at least one plastic bottle with a dispensing top (for example, an empty washing-up liquid bottle). One player is chosen to be the street painter. They squeeze the bottle, which has been filled with water, and with the water jet draw any figure or object on to the pavement. The players standing around the painter watch as the painting comes into being and try to guess what the painting could be. Each correctly guessed design earns 10 points for the observer.

This game is particularly exciting on a hot summer's day, when the sun blazes down from the sky and quickly dries off the damp trail.

Tip: The game gets more exciting if two groups compete with each other, with each group preparing cards with ideas on them for the other which must then be put into action by the painter of the opposite team.

Materials: plastic bottles with dispensing tops

(158) Sun and Sea

This game is for any number of participants, and is about concentration and ability to react.

One player says a word – for example, 'sun'. The next participant in the round now has to say quickly the first word that comes to mind when they hear 'sun': for example, 'sea'. A third player says their association with 'sea', maybe 'Italy': Italy – pizza – mozzarella – tomatoes – and so on. The game can be played in this way, with players taking turns, or randomly until no one can think of anything else – which can take quite a while.

(159) Blob Hunt

The blob hunt is a colourful catch game for fast sprinters on warm summer days. The only materials required are finger paints, a particular colour being chosen for each round. If possible, participants should be wearing swimming costumes.

One player – the catcher – dips both hands into, for example, the yellow paint pot. At the start signal, the group starts running. The hunt is on within a previously marked-off area. The blob hunter tries to give as many players as possible a yellow mark. The winner is the player who is skilful enough to get away without any yellow marks. They become the colour hunter for the next, maybe red, blob hunt.

Tip: The game becomes even more exciting if the blob has to be left on a particular part of the body (for example, the back).

Materials: finger paints

(160) Back Quiz

Back guessing is a popular game where the identities of people, professions, animals and objects have to be guessed.

The group writes the names of people, animals etc, on as many pieces of paper as there are players. These are then put face-down on the table. Everyone picks one piece of paper, without reading what is written on it. Using sticky tape, the leader fixes the piece of paper to the back of the player, who still has no idea what is written on it. Now the first candidate stands in the middle of the circle and slowly turns around. The people in the circle read the piece of paper, and then must answer the player's questions, using only 'yes' and 'no'. The player in the middle tries to find out the solution by asking questions, but they are only allowed 20 in total. If they guess the answer within this limit, they are applauded and are allowed to replace their piece of paper with another. If the answer remains undiscovered, another player tries their luck in the next round.

Tip: Initially, the game is easier if one agrees on a particular topic. For example, if the names of famous people are written down, the following questions can be useful: Am I a current celebrity? Am I male? Am I known in politics? And so on.

Materials: paper, pens, sticky tape